The Essential Online Solution

The 5-Step Formula for Small Business Success

RICK SEGEL

AND

BARBARA CALLAN-BOGIA

WILEY

John Wiley & Sons, Inc.

Published by John Wiley & Sons, Inc., Hoboken, New Jersey.
Published simultaneously in Canada.

For general information on our other products and services or for technical support, please contact our Customer Care Department within the United States at (800) 762-2974, outside the United States at (317) 572-3993 or fax (317) 572-4002.

Wiley also publishes its books in a variety of electronic formats. Some content that appears in print may not be available in electronic books. For more information about Wiley products, visit our web site at *www.wiley.com*.

Library of Congress Cataloging-in-Publication Data:

Segel, Rick.
   The essential online solution : The 5-step formula for small business success / Rick Segel and Barbara Callan-Bogia.
       p. cm.
   Includes index.
   ISBN-13: 978-0-471-92053-3 (pbk.)
   ISBN-10: 0-471-92053-3 (pbk.)
   1. Electronic commerce.   2. Small business—Computer networks.   3. Internet marketing.   I. Callan-Bogia, Barbara.   II. Title.
   HF5548.32.S445 2006
   658.8'72—dc22
                                                                          2006013972

Printed in the United States of America.

10 9 8 7 6 5 4 3 2 1

RICK SEGEL'S DEDICATION

As we go through our lives we meet a lot of people. Some we get to know quite well, and, they stay in our lives for years and years. Others float through the various periods of our lives, such as during college or some job. We think we could never live without them, but somehow we drift away. Some touch us for just an instant, but that instant can last a lifetime. This book is dedicated to someone who fits one of these brief moments in time.

The person's name is Betty Hill, and she is the owner of the Theatrical Shop in West Des Moines, Iowa. As I write, Betty is 83 give or take a year, but she doesn't look a day over 65. Betty was the first person I met who was being successful online. She became an inspiration for writing this book. Betty started her first web site when she was 79 years old and now has seven sites. When many people younger than herself were picking out retirement homes and relaxing in Florida, Betty was picking her domain names. When some people her age were trying to figure out Medicare benefits, Betty worked on search engine optimization.

You might say she did it because she had to work. On the contrary, Betty is an extremely successful businesswoman. Not only does she own the Theatrical Shop, she also owns two dance schools and several pieces of property in town as well. She is a self-made, financially independent woman who is still vital, active, and always looking for ways to improve. Age isn't a number—it's an attitude. Betty Hill has an attitude for business and living.

What Betty did was make me aware of the thousands of small businesspeople who learned that online commerce works, integrated it into their own business, and then made a business of that initiative. Thanks, Betty, for opening my eyes and sending me off on the path that created this book. My favorite expression now, when someone tells me it can't be done, is to say, "Betty did it, and she is 80." God Bless Betty Hill and all of the other Betty Hills in this world who don't say, "Why do that?" They say, "Why not?" The least I could do was dedicate this book to Betty as a thank-you for being an inspiration to the possibilities of online commerce, business, and life.

I tip my hat to you. You made a difference.

BARBARA CALLAN-BOGIA'S DEDICATION

We dedicate this book to small-business owners who have a business or are just starting out. We wish you well on your online journey. May you boost your online presence so that it converts to sales, fun, and prosperity.

This book is also dedicated to my incredible parents, Regina and Francis Callan, who helped mold me into the person I am today. Thanks, and I miss you every day.

To my mother-in-law, Ruth Bogia, who has encouraged and inspired me on this journey by her confidence in me to write this book.

To David who means the world to me. How blessed I am to have you for a soul mate and husband.

ACKNOWLEDGMENTS

A book doesn't just "show up" on the book shelves. There are many people who help, inspire, give suggestions, research, or are just there when you need them to make a book a reality. The first thanks goes to Rick's wife, Margie Segel, for her help—and for putting up with Rick during the process. We also wish to thank our agent Jeff Hermann, the consummate professional, who represented us in the most professional and ethical manner. That was very important to us.

A very special thank-you to our technical editor, Roland Lacey, president of MediaRight Technologies, for ensuring the accuracy of the content, the quality of the material, and the value of every recommendation in this book. He was our resident genius and secret weapon. We hope this book doesn't change his life too much.

We don't know if we are allowed to say nice things about our editor, but we will anyway. It was great working with David Pugh of John Wiley & Sons. His belief and enthusiasm for the book made us write the book that you now hold. Thanks for letting us be creative right up to the end and for reigning us in when we needed it. We don't know if editors are supposed to inspire, but you did with your words of encouragement.

Thanks also to Mike Black, Ali Goodwin, Paige Stover-Hague, and Paul Lubin for helping to first get this idea off the ground. Rick didn't forget you. A special thanks to Cynthia Potts, for your thoughtful ideas and contributions.

There is one other group of people that inspire us, motivate us, and have become our professional family. We call them our "Mastermind Group"—Susan Keane Baker, CSP; Margo Chevers; Margie Green; Jim Snack, CSP; and Joe Veneto. They are all professional writers and speakers and make a difference in the lives of people every day. Thanks for making a difference in our lives and helping to make this book happen. You're the best!

Lastly, but most importantly, we acknowledge our families. That is really what life is all about. We won't mention any names here because Barbara comes from a family of 9 and Rick's children and grandchildren number 10. But you will all get a copy, and none of you will pay for a single one.

CONTENTS

Chapter 1

Introduction

Ninety-five years ago a young Jewish man of 16 left a small Ukrainian village in Czarist Russia to flee from persecution and almost certain death. He had a cousin in America who sponsored him, and he was able to leave Russia to settle in the most northern part of Wisconsin. Apparently they loved cold weather!

This newcomer fathered six children. When the oldest was 18 and the youngest was only 4, he was killed in an automobile accident. Those six children lived through poverty and then all went on to become very successful beyond the wildest of dreams of that Russian immigrant.

This man did not live a distinguished life. His life was one of hard, backbreaking work as a fruit peddler with long hours. His evenings were filled with reading and studying. Very few people knew this man, but he is remembered mostly for the four simple words that he lived by and repeated to his children over and over again. The words became the mantra for his family and the battle cry of his six successful children. The words seem almost meaningless until you look at them a little closer: "It's a new America."

The words meant—and justified—the multitude of changes taking place in a growing country. Those four words also created an acceptance for change, for new ideas, and an attitude that change and innovation are part of America. They are what make America great.

So what's with this story about a Russian immigrant, and what does it have to do with a book on online solutions? What does it have to do with a book about new ways of doing more business? Everything. You are going to experience and learn new ways to market, new ways to communicate with your customers, new ways to create communities for your customers, and new ways to create loyalty. You will learn ways to become a valued resource to your customers—to have your customers become loyal by default.

You are going to learn ways to service your customers better, keep them better informed, sell them more, and discover ways to create your own word-of-mouth advertising. When you can have word-of-mouth advertising without opening your mouth, that's a change. Just click and send it—that is, what we call a *clend* (click and send)—and this how news spreads instantly.

This book is not about the hottest new fad in e-commerce, although many of the techniques will be new and innovative to many. This book is not about cutting edge technology, although it will appear cutting edge to many.

So why do we say that the fruit peddler from Russia has everything to do with online solutions? Because many of you will read and understand some of the concepts you are about to learn, but you will fight the changes. You will reject them just as many people rejected new ideas during those days of the fruit peddler. Many of you will not push yourself through the learning stage to make the concept work.

Before you are overwhelmed, there are three very important components about this book. First, it is not written by techies, engineers, or computer nerds. On the contrary, it is written by two businesspeople who are business trainers and authors. They will focus on what these new techniques and processes will do for the business rather then focusing on how they work. As far as we are concerned it's magic, but even great magicians concentrate on their results.

Second, we are going to highlight accepted proven products, processes, techniques, and procedures. Although many people look at these new ways of doing business as cutting edge, they are not. We don't want the next great idea that hasn't been tested in this book.

This book is about harnessing the power of the best and easiest tools available on the market today. This book is about getting started or becoming more effective with your online endeavors. It's also about making money online. We are marketing people, and the online world has become a virtual cornucopia of new marketing concepts.

For the record, the way we evaluate any of the ideas, concepts, or tools is by asking if it first works and if it was easy to use. It's not about all the features—just show us the benefits.

Last point is the most difficult. Technology is changing faster than ever before. So because of that we concentrate on the concept or the Big Picture rather than the latest software release, which would only be out of date by the time this book is published. An example would be the concept of *blogging*. Blogging is here to stay—but the server software that makes blogging happen might change.

So let's begin our journey of discovery to uncover the secrets of online solutions, because it's not just a new America today. It is a new world, where change is the currency of the day and the old promise of streets paved with gold is still alive and well, just as they were for Rick's grandfather, the fruit peddler from Russia. The streets paved with gold are there for every entrepreneur on the virtual streets of the technology highway as long as you are willing to use the awesome power of online solutions. Get ready—it's going to be fun and very, very profitable.

Chapter 1's Essential Essentials

1. Be open to learning lots of possibilities for your online business.
2. Get a notepad—on paper or on your PC—to record all the great ideas you discover and don't want to lose as you read and apply what you have learned.
3. Take a deep breath and have fun!

For more information on this topic, go to
www.essentialonlinesolution.com.

Step I

Uncovering the Possibilities

Chapter 2

Online Business Solutions

Where Are We At?
Understanding the Past, Present, and Future of Online Business

We started to learn about the Internet in the early 1990s, although it had been around a lot longer. By 1995, we learned what WWW meant worldwide web and began to hear predictions that it would change the way we live and do business. New businesses started to pop up. Web designing became an industry. Someone with two years' experience creating web sites was referred to as a seasoned pro. The big concern early on was how people were going to find you online. Obviously that was before Google and Yahoo. Then came the onslaught of Internet-only businesses. In the late 1990s, it seemed that the whole world would be buying everything online. From furniture to pet food, everything was being sold online. It was the age of the *Dot Com*. We got Internet drunk.

Wall Street started throwing money at Internet startups that frankly didn't deserve it. Companies that were losing money were getting millions of dollars in the hopes that they would eventually make money. The problem was with the word *eventually*. What investors perceived as eventually and what it would actually take were two different timetables. Unfortunately, investors couldn't wait and the exodus began.

Overreaction has always been the M.O. of Wall Street. Understand that widespread Internet use is less than 10 years old; that's when Netscape introduced the first browser. Growth has been nothing short of phenomenal. Customers are feeling more and more secure about purchasing online and they are doing it in record numbers every year. Yet online businesses still only represents the minority of total revenues produced. Having said that, there are some industries that have become dominated by online methods. The travel business—think Travelocity—is one of them, as is the legendary success of *Amazon.com* in books and media and *Monster.com* in the personnel business.

Yet with all the successful online retail businesses that exist today, it still only represents less than 10 percent of total retail sales. We are still in the infancy of a transformation of buying patterns.

Is it too late to enter the online world of e-commerce? No. And it's never too late to enter a business if your idea is unique enough, your marketing is clever enough, and your execution is good enough. But having said all of that, we are living in the most fertile time of online development because we now have a history of successful best practices and models. *You might have missed the ground floor of e-commerce, but you also missed the trapdoors in the floor that destroyed many businesses.* We have learned how to do it, how to run a successful online business, and how to avoid the pitfalls while still leaving plenty of room for growth and boundless opportunity.

To use the Gold Rush analogy, we missed the first strikes, but now we know where we should look for gold, what tools to use, and the things we should or shouldn't do. We are benefiting from others' mistakes and successes.

What is the promise for the independent businessperson? It is the ability of exposing your business to the world at very little cost. It is increasing your base of potential customers/clients from just your marketing area to the world. Big deal—we all know that but businesses could always do that! All you had to do was start a business through the mail or via the phones. You could buy a list of potential customers and send catalogs and brochures and hope that they would respond and eventually buy. The Internet and doing business online has changed all of that because of speed and costs.

Let's talk about the cost savings. You don't have to pay for the printing or the mailing. You will even know when someone doesn't receive the mail, and it won't cost you a cent. The promise of e-commerce coincided with digital everything and desktop publishing that not only save you money on printing and mailing but on designing and photography. We now have web document templates for almost any kind of design you can imagine. Boring is out because all of these templates are beyond affordable—they are downright cheap. You can purchase 500 web design templates for $29.95. Just a few short years ago a custom-designed site could cost $10,000+ and now some of the current templates are far superior to those designs. The moons are in perfect alignment. We have reached the tipping point. We have reached the point where doing business is easy enough and cheap enough for the world to participate.

THERE ARE TWO SIDES OF THE ONLINE REVOLUTION

The two sides of the online way of doing business are the front end and the back end: marketing and sales on the front end and processing the transaction on the back end. As an example, we'll use a training business. It markets its business in different ways online, which we discuss in later chapters. But that's only half of the magic. This business can also deliver its training in a downloadable format.

A retailer can attract business, take an order, and have all the receipts, follow-ups, and even electronically order from a supplier and have it drop ship directly to the customer. The retailer never has to take possession of the product.

Rick has three books that are downloadable online. The publisher doesn't have to print them, bind them, ship them, or even handle any complaints that they were damaged during shipment. Do you think there is a savings there? Do you think margins are healthy? Before you even think in terms of price gouging, let's think about what's in it for the customers. They get the book instantly. That process alone has increased Rick's foreign sales over 600% because the information becomes not only immediate but without the red tape of shipping, duty, tariffs, the risk of loss, and the extra time that whole process takes.

Although this book is primarily focused on the front-end side of online commerce, we must realize the true cost benefits might be from the back end. The airlines don't need as many reservationists because these companies have encouraged—and threatened—their customers to buy tickets online. The airlines encourage travelers by offering extra points in their frequent flyer programs. American offers 500 points for buying online; but it charges $10 if the traveler buys his or her ticket on the phone through a reservationist.

MORE GOOD NEWS—IT'S ALL ABOUT THE SPEED

Online businesses have opened new doors because of the speed and quality of the information. You can make a great buy in the morning, tell your customers you have something they need in the early afternoon, and receive orders before 4:00 P.M.—before the merchandise comes in the next morning. Better than that is you don't have to take possession of the merchandise You can get paid for merchandise before you get an invoice. If you are selling services, it gets even better. Think of which online solutions have touched almost every industry in the world. New applications are only limited by one's imagination and desire. The sacred cows of industry are being slain. Entire sales processes are being converted into online solutions daily. Who would have thought the neighborhood yard sale could be replaced by an online auction site?

ONLINE SOLUTIONS ARE A NEW WAY TO MARKET

Think about this: We, as business people, have a new way to market to both potential and existing customers. Online solutions have become the new basic in marketing. The exciting part is that within the online world there are many different ways to solve today's marketing challenges. We have progressed from selling from carts to storefronts with free and ample parking, catalogs, home parties, telemarketing, fax marketing, TV shopping networks, and now the fastest and least expensive of them all—e-commerce. It is the promise of a new platform to sell our goods and services. That alone would be sufficient, but there is more.

The Online World Creates New Ways to Communicate to Your Customers and Build Relationships

There was always face to face, the mail, or the telephone call. Now we have added e-mail, e-zines, instant messaging, text messaging, informing our customers or clients about promotions, a new products, techniques, new arrivals, previews of what's coming in, changes in the industry, how to best use the product, or even just topics of interest to our customers. Again, doing it faster and cheaper than all of the rest. To say that we are just communicating with our customer is an understatement, because we are getting our customer involved with our business—we are creating an interactive community.

Rick recently experienced the power of creating a community when he spoke for a group that he has spoken at before. Many of the attendees read Rick's weekly free business tip that is e-mailed to them every Tuesday morning. As he shared an experience in story form, people in the audience started nodding their heads as if to say, "We read that in your column and it does make sense." Online initiatives can make things obsolete very quickly because we are communicating in real time.

When we communicate better, our relationships build. It's all about keeping in touch with our customers and following up on the things that are important to them. Communicating better is knowing more about customers than ever before, what they like, when they usually buy it, and what price is the right price. It is about the friendly reminders that pinpoint our customers and build relationships. It's not about sending generic pieces or blind messages to the masses. It's about low cost, highly effective personalization to our community. That's what online solutions for business are all about. It's about keeping in touch almost effortlessly.

Online Solutions Are a New Way to Price and Present Our Goods and Services

If there is one single universal error that businesses make, it is not stopping to see what their competition is doing. The bigger the business, the bigger the teams that spy on—or *shop*—the competition. We know the word *"spy"* is a bit rough; but that's really what it is. Plumbers don't always shop other web sites for plumbers, but they should. Most smaller businesses will do it occasionally but rarely on a regular basis. Obviously, in years past, it wasn't the easiest thing to do. Today there is no excuse. That's what the online world has done for pricing and presentation. You can see what other people in your industry are doing, what you like, what you dislike, what could work for you.

You can even go on eBay to see if similar items appear and what they are selling for.

Let customers decide the price they want to pay. Auctions have allowed the business to do just that. Yes, auctions are an integral element of e-commerce that should and are being included in almost every business's online initiatives. Isn't that the simplest and purest way to price? What someone is willing to pay for something is the right price to sell it at. We can obtain presentation and pricing information easily online and seamlessly integrate the information into our business.

Online Solutions Are Another Market to Expand Business

Online solutions provide an additional income opportunity for the independent that never existed before. It is like having a new housing development expand near your business or a major employer move into your town. Politicians fight to have economic development take place in their communities and many are starting to realize the bonanza online businesses can have for the local economy.

Now a business can double or triple its business without having to open more locations. Overexpansion has been the major culprit for the demise of many good businesses. But the online world allows safe expansion with limited risks. It allows specialists to thrive with the giants.

Just as the super highway made our customers more mobile and allowed them to travel to the big box, the mall, or three towns over to shop, e-commerce expands the highway through technology. It makes the commute to your store from distant places possible and instantaneous. "Scottie, beam me up" can now be applied to a shopping trip. We used to brag about our businesses if we were able to draw customers from four or five surrounding towns. Then it became cool to say they come from other states. But now small retailers brag about doing business in 15 or 20 different countries!

You can now sell to the world. The retailer's store window is now located on the super highway for the world to see. E-commerce can offer the housing development, the new industry in town, and the store window for every business willing to learn about it.

Online Solutions Represent Better Service to Your Customers

For the last two decades we have focused on serving our customers better. But good customer service is different things to different people. The online world personalizes the level of customer service you want. I can check my own delivery status. I can reorder when I want or when I am reminded by an electronically generated e-mail. If you forget a password it can be sent to you instantaneously. I don't even have to go to the Registry of Motor Vehicles because it is all done online.

Think about what is now taking place: Better, faster service that is costing less to offer with less human involvement. Having said that, you can still have a real person to field questions but you don't need as many, and most people prefer the control that the online world brings to the table.

The Online World Is the Promise of Going Into Business for Yourself

The entry-level financial requirements are relatively small and success is determined more by know-how than just financial strengths. The thrill, joy, and pride of business ownership is one of the greatest feelings in the world. Not having to be dependent on someone else is utopia. Not worrying about a decision made by others to close the plant or to get laid off is worth much more than money.

Online Solutions Are a New Hope for Downtowns

Rick spends half of his professional life working on downtown revitalization projects. Downtowns across America have been devastated by hypercompetition. But online solutions can allow downtown merchants to thrive with fewer customers walking through the front door as long as packages are being shipped out the back door. Lower rents of the downtown are now more appealing because location is not as important as sufficient space and shipping capabilities. Downtowns are starting to thrive because of e-commerce and online solutions.

Online Solutions Are about Getting Rich

Yes, there are many people who are making more money than they ever could imagine due to online solutions. We have lived through a generation or two where being an independent businessperson meant making a living. Some made a good living, but rich? That was only for a select few. E-commerce and online initiatives can generate substantial incomes for anyone who is willing to learn the tricks of the trade. Independent retailers haven't been able to say that in decades. Years ago the richest people in town were the retailers. That is about to happen again. No, this book isn't intended to be a get-rich-quick book but we are sure there will be people buying it for that purpose and we will be offering the tools to succeed. But it is more than just money. It is about the opportunities that e-commerce brings which allow us to live a life beyond our stores, with our families and loved ones. We don't have to be working every waking moment because we have a shop open, making us money, even when we are sleeping. The online solution is about financial freedom and that just leads to a change in us.

We almost used "The Good, The Bad and The Ugly" to describe this chapter and the origins of e-commerce and online solutions. But we have saved that expression for another chapter. And we really question if there really were bad or ugly parts. Sure, in retrospect, the failures were terrible but each mistake brought us closer to today's accepted steps of online success. Besides, we wonder sometimes if the biggest failures just needed a little more time to develop. Our job, and the job of this book, is to shorten the learning curve to online success. It's time to start to master it. Let's begin.

Chapter 2's Essential Essentials

1. Don't reinvent the wheel. Learn from others' mistakes so you can catch the second wave of Internet commerce.
2. An online business can save you money with many new opportunities especially when it comes to advertising, publishing, and the like.
3. Online business is all about speed.
4. Online solutions are a new way to price and present goods and services.
5. Online solutions are another market in which to expand business.
6. Online solutions represent better service to your customers.
7. The online world is the promise of going into business for yourself.
8. Online solutions are about getting rich.

For more information on this topic, go to

www.essentialonlinesolution.com.

Chapter 3

Why Do People Buy Online?

What Motivates Them?

The strange thing about this chapter title is the instant reaction people have when we discuss why we buy online. People become very opinionated, emphatic, and even stubborn about their reason and everyone believes they are right. Some automatically say price. Others say "It's easier." Some say, "It's fun." And the insomniacs and overworked say they can shop in the middle of the night. E-commerce and specifically buying online represent different things to different people. We all have different motivations and they are all justified. It is almost a "Tastes Great or Less Filling" controversy. No one is wrong and everybody is right.

However, traditional marketing tells us that there are two basic ways to define our customers and clients: either with *demographics*—the statistical information of who our customers are, or *psychographics*—the life styles information of what our customers

17

do. The online world has clearly made a strong case for a new category that we refer to as *Motographics* or the motivation for why we buy what we buy.

Certainly, demographic and psychographic information can be an indicator of one's motivation; but *Motographics* is the actual reason that the sale or transaction occurs. Are we splitting hairs a bit? Yes, but with today's technology we have the ability and information to be able to microniche a market, or what we like to refer to as "niche within a niche, within a niche..."

It is important to understand these motivations or reasons before we design our online business. We need to first decide what buying motivation group or groups we are appealing to, because this will change the way we do things and why we do things. You will begin to see what I mean as we discuss the various reasons. Many are the same reasons our clients or customers already do business with us but because of the unique qualities of online buying, the motivations either change or strengthen. A convenience buyer, someone that is motivated by the currency of time, will love the online experience only if it has a perception of saving time. One-click shopping at Amazon was made for this form of motivation.

Let's look now at some of the biggest motivators.

THE PRICE MOTIVATION

It all started here. Go online and you can save money. We all looked at the reduced level of operating expenses and said it only makes sense that something would be cheaper online. No expensive locations, no salespeople, fewer employees, and you can be open 24/7. It made sense that prices would be cheaper. To further justify that way of thinking, there was a sense of risk in the beginning in relation to security. That only forwarded the belief that the prices must be cheaper. Before you question risk, let's not forget that greed and money are powerful. Then throw in the thrill of the hunt. You were putting your credit card information online to a vendor that had only been in business a few months. We weren't even sure we would get the merchandise let alone have our identity or credit card stolen. As dangerous as that might have sounded, it all added to the lower price mystique.

Now shopping BOTS such as Google's Froogle have arrived, which search the web for the lowest-price vendor online. This has its advantages and obvious disadvantages. The advantages are that a little-known business can get noticed by the world if it chooses to become the lowest-price provider. Yes, you will probably do business that way but can you make money that way and is it the type of business you really want to be? Do you want to build your business with just price?

Every business, however, needs that promotable item, and if you are using price to lure them to your business so that you can *wow* them with speed, reliability, or service, then it has its place. It is not hard to believe that we would go online originally for the savings. Many people believe it is the purpose of the web: to save the consumer money and to be the low-cost alternative. The goal is to build a customer base. Don't try to do it with just price because the customer it attracts is not loyal to you but rather your low prices. If someone is cheaper, then you are history.

Although e-commerce has its roots as the low-price alternative, it has come a long way from those days. Remember, you are entering the online world after the first two waves of the infantry have hit the beaches. A path exists for us and fighting the price wars is full of landmines that have been the demise of many of the first wave of online businesses.

How Do You Appeal to the Price Customer?

Before you answer that, ask yourself the question, "Why would you want to appeal to the price buyer?" If you are in the business of "deals" or discount or off-price merchandise, then you embrace that customer. But, as opposed to the traditional channels of doing business, don't try to fool customers because they can comparison shop in seconds. *Live by price and you will die by price.* The problem is the buyer is only loyal to the price, not you, unless you can *wow* them in another way. Southwest Airlines, which made its mark with low prices and fun, added an additional differentiator that has become as important as the price and that is a web site that is so easy to understand and use. You scroll through a list of cities Southwest Airlines flies to and from, and the site lists all of the available flight times and a choice of fares. By making its web site easy to use, Southwest was able to differentiate itself from competing airlines that had begun matching it on price.

Enough with this word of caution. To attract the price customer, you must show the best deals on the home page. Create a series of small space bordered ads with pictures of the product, the selling price, and the value. Create a "Hot Deal" on every page. Make sure you are constantly changing your site, updating it daily. Ask for the types of deals customers are looking for, offer pinpointed e-mails about their interests. Bundle the products with various price propositions such as "Buy 2 Get 1 Free," "Buy 1 Get Second Half Price," and "Buy three or more and take an additional 20 percent off." Offer a gift certificate for your next purchase or a free gift with purchase that can be a logo T-shirt or hat from your business. Avoid just a single low price on a single item. You are much better off by offering value packages. We would rather make a small margin on two items than just one. Value customers are price customers who tend to be more loyal to your business. After all, they generally have more of your products.

THE RESEARCH MOTIVATION

This was definitely the second motivation for the earlier online shopper. Let your fingers do the walking. Shop 20 different businesses in an hour and you could become a better-informed consumer. As this trend was developing, businesses would joke that customers would know more about what they sell than they do. That part hasn't changed, but the difference between now and then is that in the past, the customer would physically shop the business or at least call the business during the times the business was open. Today, however, the customer eliminates the additional step since trust of the online business has increased, security features were instituted, and remedies were put in place.

How Do You Appeal to the Research Customer?

Understanding that customers shop you for information, it is important to plan our e-commerce initiatives with information, knowledge about our products, ways to use it, and a continuing source of that degree of expertise. That is why it is critical for most online businesses to offer regular newsletters or e-zines or e-mails that solely focus on educating the consumer. Position your business as the expert and you will have more traffic than you can handle. We pay extra for expertise. We can justify that premium in our minds.

THE CONVENIENCE MOTIVATOR

The power of convenience won the web. Any time we can make things easier and faster, it always beats out the alternative. For example, we can all buy a five-year-old computer that is dirt cheap and probably very reliable. But do you really want to wait 40 seconds to change programs? If you have been working with a high-speed connection and have to use a dial up, you are willing to spend almost anything for a high-speed broadband connection. That's why hotels can charge $10 or $12 a day for a high-speed Internet connection.

It's easier to go online to look for a specific product without having to waste time driving to or even hunting for the business on phone. Besides why hassle with parking the car or shopping various places when it can all be done with just a few clicks from home? But that's only the beginning of convenience. What about shopping at 3:00 A.M in your bathrobe? That's convenience.

When we get an e-mail from a business that informs us that the item that we are looking for just came in, like Amazon does with specific books we like to read, that's convenience. When we shop at a site and it recommends alternatives to the selection off to the side, that's convenience. Just go to Land's End and pick out a pair of chinos. The site will make suggestions based on what you have chosen. It is helpful, and many times we will buy the suggestions. They are saving us time, serving us better, while increasing the vendor's business.

When we can go online to a business we buy from regularly, it has all of our pertinent information, including credit card information, on file and all we have to do is a fast click. That's convenience. One of us recently bought a book on Amazon in less than one minute from start to finish. That is why convenience is winning on the web.

The key question we must constantly ask ourselves is, is our business as easy and user friendly as possible? As discussed earlier, look at the Southwest Airlines web site. It is so simple and easy to use that you wonder why other airlines don't utilize its model.

We can build a business without the best product, without the lowest price, but by being the most convenient. Convenience is *king*. Master it and you will be well on your way to online success.

How Do You Appeal to the Convenience Customer?

Review every exposure or touch your company has with the customer. It has been referred to as the moment of truth or the moment of magic. From searching for what you sell to opening your web site, convenience is the ability to find what the customer is looking for as quickly and easily as possible. There is a concept called the *minimum level of professionalism,* which refers to having a web site that looks good but doesn't have all of the fancy openings with music and pictures. Yes, these sites are beautiful but most people are opting to shut them off for a quick loading, tell me what you are selling site. That's what convenience means.

Review your process to buy. Is it fast, easy, and does it make sense? What about the way the merchandise or product is shipped? And are you making the process to send something back easy? Some businesses like to make customers jump through hoops to get a refund or a resolution to a problem. Please don't—it only hurts everyone and affects the trust factor of the web. Make everything user friendly and easy to use.

THE CONTROL MOTIVATION

Have you ever had a slow-moving cashier? You feel like screaming because you could ring up the sale faster yourself. Do you remember talking to an airline reservationist who is new and just learning? It drives us crazy. E-commerce lets us drive the car, make the reservation, pick out the size, the color, which credit card we want to use—and if we are over our limit on a card, we don't have to hear this moron tell us our card is bad in front of a store full of customers. It lets us decide what we want, when we want it, at a price we want to buy it, without some minimum-wage clerk, who doesn't want to be there to begin with, bothering us. Then you add anonymity to the control issue, and you will see why many people would rather do it themselves.

How Do You Appeal to the Control Motivated?

This is simple—give them control. Make it so that customers interface with no one. Allow them to make the decision. Offer a pull-down help menu—something they can figure out for themselves. To cement this relationship, reward their efforts. Offer perks or discounts for taking control. The best examples of capturing control customers are the airlines when they give 1,000 extra reward miles for booking online. What can you give your customers for buying without assistance? Have the assistance ready, but rarely will control customers use it.

THE SPECIALTY MOTIVATION

We go online to find businesses that specialize in a specific product. We are living in the age of specialists. We want the unique, the different, that specialty item not owned by everyone else. This is where the online business shines. We don't go to a regular doctor; we go to the specialist. We need to develop our niche. The jeweler that goes online with 5,000 different items doesn't always do as well as the jeweler that just sells belly button rings. The reason for that is when we shop the web we tend to search by a specific product.

That is why there is a growing trend to have multiple web sites all specializing in a specific product rather than a catch-all web site. For example, a costume shop has a site for just Santa Claus suits because the customer is more apt to search for Santa suits than costume shop because that is the exact item he or she wants.

How Do You Appeal to the Specialty Buyer?

This is where the keyword search and pay per click reign. The more you can define and verbalize your product's uniqueness, the stronger your business will become. This is not quite as simple as it might sound because of one roadblock: it's not how we define our product, it's the way our customers define our products. A jeweler may think he sells unique time pieces but the customer is searching for unique watches. We will be discussing searching in later chapters but the lesson to be learned at this juncture is that the online world has become the first choice for finding the unusual, unique, and different and there are ways to tell the world about your niche.

THE TRUST MOTIVATION

The web didn't start off that way but it is becoming an important factor. Whoever would have thought that a feeling of security, safety, and trust would be a motivating factor? People pay extra money for security and peace of mind. But it is simply safer to go online to buy than ever before. We no longer question the trust, but if you create the wrong web presence you can destroy your online business's trust. The merchandise gets delivered right to your door. But what has made trust a leading motivator is a no-hassle return policy. Every web merchant knows that if you make the returns too difficult, customers will lose that trust. That is why many merchants include return instructions and labels with every purchase. Every time I see that I feel secure about doing business with that company.

There are just three simple words that create trust and safety online. *Guarantees, guarantees, and guarantees.* Will there be people who will take advantage of that? Yes. But don't focus on them.

Focus on the bigger picture and chalk them up to a cost of doing business.

EMOTIONAL CONNECTION MOTIVATORS

Yes, we get attached to certain sites. We feel comfortable there; we get used to where everything is, just as in a brick-and-mortar world. We have a sense of belonging to a site. When was the last time you tried to change your home page on your Internet browser? You just weren't comfortable with the change. That is why we can't make too many changes too quickly. Be careful of making changes because your site creates connections that keep customers coming back. When the site makes it to a favorite list, then we have created a pattern or habit that can be part of an everyday activity. Sites can create connections just like people.

How Do You Appeal to the Emotional Customer?

Add the personal touch to your site. Tell your company history, show pictures of employees, include the mission or vision statement about your business. Talk about your charitable endeavors and why someone should do business with you. Offer contests that allow you to get to know your customers or clients better. We will discuss more of these marketing efforts in later chapters. The key overriding belief here is to put a face, a real person, behind the monitor and you will reach a different level of connection with your customer.

ENTERTAINMENT

For many people shopping online is fun. It is the thrill of the hunt. It is the challenge of finding that certain item online. Rick, while writing this book, broke a metal hinge from a corner cabinet in the kitchen. It could not use any universal hinge; it had to fit just right. Since the cabinets came with the house, there was no way to know who installed them. The brand name was illegible. Without this hinge he and his wife would have to have a new cabinet made to match the others. That could be expensive. Within 10 minutes, however, his wife found the right hinge online and purchased it for $6.79. What was more important than the financial savings was the challenge and thrill of finding the item. *That's entertainment.*

Research may not be fun for everyone. Nevertheless, some people love window-shopping online—which is really like window-shopping on steroids. Online you can tour a house or watch a video clip. Surfing the web can kill time better than anything ever created and it gives a business a new platform to have fun and market, too. You can display your funny ads, comical signs, or even create characters for comic relief. Make it fun and they will come.

Retailer Story

A leading camera shop in the Boston area has had a policy for years that offered a $5 allowance toward a new camera to any customers who brought in their old and even broken cameras. The store looked at this promotion as a little price incentive and an encouragement to purchase a new camera. This store was known for its extensive inventory and for the best prices around, and a $5 incentive was a big deal.

The store took the used cameras and put them on a table with a sign "$5 ANY CAMERA." This practice continued success-fully for over 25 years.

The store had become very successful utilizing eBay auctions and eventually hired full-time employees just to work in the eBay

---

Retailer Story, continued

department. One of these new employees commented that the store should put the $5 cameras on eBay. The owner responded with a disgusted and demeaning reply stating that he wasn't going to pay this person's salary to waste time on eBay for a $5 camera. He felt that there is no real value there. He looked at the customer only as a price customer.

The owner doesn't really remember how some of these $5 cameras made it to eBay, but somehow they did—and did they sell! But they didn't sell for the $5 price. They sold for more, getting $15, $20, $30, and as much as $175 for one camera. The owner was shocked and in total disbelief. However, they sold because they had that value to someone. Mostly collectors bought them—people who had researched and searched for specific items for their collections. They were not buying a cheap camera. They were buying a piece of history, a memory, something that no one had. This was totally opposite from the thinking of the store owner who thought it was all about price.

This experience not only sold cameras but it changed the focus of some of the other offerings because they saw for the first time another customer that they never realized ever existed. Find a niche and you'll get rich!

MAJOR MOTIVATORS

These are the major motivators in capsule form that must be considered and addressed before you begin your online venture. Brainstorm every motivator and look for ways that you can incorporate the concepts to make your e-business responsive to your customers. But remember this is only a partial list of the biggest motivators. We all buy for some of the craziest reasons.

- Price
- Research
- Convenience
- Control
- Specialists
- Trust
- Emotional Connection
- Entertainment

PRACTICE SESSION: YOUR MAJOR MOTIVATORS

Exercise One: Make a list of your major motivators.

_____

_____

_____

_____

_____

_____

_____

_____

_____

_____

_____

_____

Exercise Two: Now make a list of what you think your ideal customer's major motivators are.

_____

_____

_____

_____

_____

_____

_____

_____

_____

_____

When you are finished, review the two lists. Are they the same and in the same order? If not, what have you learned that will help you make the E-commerce Promise pay off?

_____

_____

_____

_____

_____

_____

_____

_____

_____

_____

Are the motivators the same for online and brick-and-mortar customers? How are you planning on addressing any differences?

_____

_____

_____

_____

_____

_____

_____

_____

_____

_____

Chapter 3's Essential Essentials

1. Is your online business focused on the Motographics or the motivation of why your customers buy online?
2. Know the type of motivation that draws customers to your site.
3. To attract the price customer, you must show the best deals on the home page. The 2 for 1 Deal, Buy Now, and the like.
4. To service the research customer, position your business as the expert by featuring lots of articles, resources, and information.
5. For your convenience customer, make everything user friendly and easy to use. Remember: minimal professionalism.
6. The control customer needs to buy without assistance. Make every user-interface action easy for them to do.
7. Specialty buyers need you to define and verbalize your product's uniqueness.
8. Emotional connection customers are looking for a face, a real person behind the monitor. Personalize your web site, tell your story, have a contest, and so on.

Chapter 3's Essential Essentials, *continued*

9. For the entertainment customer have fun. Use fun icons, entertaining captions, and sidebars. Show video clips, or include jokes and cartoons in your e-zines. Utilize fun and creative uses of humor to elevate the web experience.

10. Look for ways that you can incorporate the customer motivational concepts to make your e-business responsive to your customers.

For more information on this topic, go to

www.essentialonlinesolution.com.

Chapter 4

The Big Picture

The Levels of Online Commerce

I have audio, video, autoresponders, a really cool intro Flash page designed by the best in the business."

So what?

Like anything in life, some people use their level of online involvement as a status symbol and one-upmanship. We did not write this chapter for the sake of bragging rights. Each business needs to understand where it is, where it should be, and where it wants to be. People can be very successful at the lowest level we describe in this chapter, Level One of online commerce. We would much rather see a site reach its full potential as opposed to wasting resources on the latest gizmo that will not return an investment—or hurt business.

It's a good time to mention once again the term *minimal level of professionalism*, which will be explained in detail later. What you need to know now is that once you reach a certain level of professionalism, anything above that level shows minimum returns on investment. The best example of that is a Flash page with music and animation designed to *wow*. However, because it frustrates web convenience, it is an annoyance. Therefore, in our description of levels, we don't give extra credit because someone has a slick, animated intro page. Why? Most people click the *Skip Intro* button.

On the opposite end, there are a number of business organizations such as Chambers of Commerce, Associations, and Main Street organizations that provide small web sites for each of their members. We refer to this as *first-generation web presence*. Once upon a time businesspeople thought they were online if they had this single business card-type web site. Of course, they were; but just as that Flash intro page can waste time and possibly money, these business card pages scream rookie and unprofessional.

Before we get hate mail from every association that ever provided this type of service, let's recognize that these basic web sites serve as the springboard to exceptional online presence for many online businesses.

As we go through the levels of online commerce, you must ask yourself the question: "What would the next level do for me?" It's a subtle shift from "I'm doing business here and let's keep it here."

Let us cite one example before we begin.

Rick's son-in-law is a plumber. While writing this book, he has used his son-in-law not only as a model but as a strong reference point to the needs of small businesses. At this writing, Osborne Plumbing in Wilmington, Massachusetts, is a two-month-old business. Yet Keith Osborne is a bright-college-degreed master plumber who has worked on some of the most prestigious buildings and development projects in the city of Boston. An important goal for his startup business is to have a Level One web presence, the most basic level in online commerce.

Keith wanted his contact information and service capabilities online. But Rick challenged Keith to look at the next level—where his web site offers helpful hints and tips to potential clients. Rick also asked what products Keith could sell online to homeowners and contractors. Keith recommended a type of plunger that's the most effective, smallest, and easiest to use he'd ever seen. Now he is considering a site that has a basic shopping cart function that allows him to market and sell the super-duper plunger. Will the plunger return millions of dollars to Osborne Plumbing? Probably not. But by offering that product, he has helped to differentiate his new business. Bottom-line—look at the level you are at and ask what the next level could bring to your business.

LEVELS OF ONLINE COMMERCE

There are various levels of commitment and involvement to online commerce. Let's walk through the various levels—but understand this is not an exact science. There are no firm boundaries and there are gray areas. This is perhaps a nice way of saying that there are different combinations of elements that can be used in the various levels.

Level One: Getting Started on the Web

This level is generally a do-it-yourself web site from the larger domain register services such as *GoDaddy.com* or *Register.com*. You yourself or a web site service provider can set it up inexpensively. It should contain:

- A five-page brochure-like web site that contains five total web pages with navigation between the pages.
- The benefits that you offer your customers.
- A description of what you do for the customer.
- Testimonials from clients.
- Contact information, that is, an e-mail account with the name of the site in the account such as *Keith@Osborneplumbing. com.*

The cost for the design and hosting of a site such as this is generally less than $20 per month. There are many places, which we will discuss in a later chapter, where you can go to have your site hosted. This is the great entry-level position. As far as design is concerned, there is an almost unlimited supply of web site templates on the web.

Level Two: I'm More Than a Rookie

In this level you are getting in the game. You are adding more functionality to your site and recognizing that this is a viable business model. This level of online commerce is comprised of:

- More than one e-mail account.
- More testimonials.
- Ten web pages or more.
- Navigation tabs (between 5 and 7) that will open to a subcategory that will have a page or two of information such as About Us, Contact Us, Services, where you describe your company and services in more detail.
- *Search Engine Optimization* (SEO), which is done by the site owner or the service that you've purchased. SEO is a way to help people on the web find your site and to have it rank higher in search engines.

- A way to collect the e-mail addresses of potential customers. This is worth doing at Level One, too. Businesses are always in the name collection business and no matter what online level you choose, you need as much data as possible. We believe the acid test is what the business owner does with this information. If he or she is not going to use it, why expect people to fill out an online form?
- A merchant account to take credit card information and shopping cart orders online.
- A shopping cart. This is a major differentiator from Level One's features. It is a simple utilitarian package that various services will charge you less then $20 a month to maintain.

The average cost to this level will run about $46 a month. Businesses can stay at Level One for a long time. Level Two is a transitional level, where businesses grow and move to Level Three.

Level Three: You Are a Player

The biggest transition to Level Three is that the majority of businesses use a professional company to manage the web site and design. Level Three sites are professional looking and may have the following features:

- 40 to 80 pages in the web site. Sites in this category can be lengthy. *GoDaddy.com* and other service providers offer premium packages that can be this big.
- Professional company-managed web site and design.
- Search Engine Optimization (SEO) that may involve having a premium version of an SEO or hiring an SEO company.
- Branded e-mails, a form of web site marketing.
- E-zine, an online magazine.

- Auto-responders. These are automated programmed responses to online requests.
- Pay-per-Click, a form of advertising.
- Online forms for clients and potential clients to supply information.
- Fulfillment procedures to handle online orders.
- E-mail and web site statistics.
- Blog. A blog, or web log, is a running journal of entries that businesses can use to maintain close contact with customers and potential customers.
- eBay auctions. This depends on the type of business. There are some businesses that are built around eBay. We are not talking about that type of business. We are talking about a traditional business that can use eBay as either an additional source of revenue or an additional marketing tool.

Level Three is the level that people stay in for a long period of time. Many people have their service needs met at this level. There is no reason to go on to the next level—or even use all of the elements listed in Level Three.

The costs vary and depend on the type of supplier you hire, its level of success, and what you're willing to spend. We think there would be a low of $150 to a high of $2,000 to $3,000 a month. However this is what we talked about at the beginning, the shades of gray, because of the different levels within each element.

Level Four: Minding Your Cash Machine

Level Four does everything that Level Three does but adds some or all of the following features:

- Flash animation. This means using it effectively—not in the introduction of home page per se, but used in building useful features for the web site itself such as drop-down menus, order forms, popups, and the like.

- Audio and video feeds.
- E-mail and web site statistical data are read, analyzed, and acted upon.
- Podcasting, a viable marketing initiative that utilizes radio broadcast-like presentations.
- RSS feeds. These bypass e-mail and allow customers to view your blog seamlessly.

This is another transitional stage. If you are here, you are on your way to Level Five. The only thing holding you back is the growth of your business.

The interesting thing is that there is not a significant cost leap from Level Three to Level Four. The real jump comes at Level Five.

Level Five: Welcome to the Big Leagues

Level Five can have everything that Level Four has. However, the major difference is the level of sophistication. Companies that are at this level have dedicated people to create and maintain their online presence and online marketing. The other major differentiator in this level is that web sites become customer service vehicles as well—and they are far more interactive. This is where clients can retrieve or access information about the products you sell or the service you provide.

- Employ information technology (IT) professionals.
- Track information.
- Help sections.
- Customer service issues.

- Discussion boards.
- Cookie technology. This means that your business web site can issue cookies (cookies can be enabled using any language) to your clients, which can be stored on their PCs. The cookie then personalizes each return visit to that web site. If your browser permits cookies, you may have noticed, say at *Amazon.com*, that it welcome's you back on a first-name basis. For example, "Welcome back, Dave."

We do not go into much detail about this level. Level Five is geared to large business such as major catalogs companies (think L.L. Bean), airline ticket sellers (think Travelocity), and the like.

Chapter 4's Essential Essentials

1. Select the desired level based on the size and complexity of your business. Do you want to progress beyond?
2. Understand what it takes to transition to the next level and what effect it will have on your business.
3. Along with additional costs come additional time and resource commitments. Are they justifiable, and when?
4. Never just utilize technology for technology's sake. If it works for you, use it. If not, it could hurt.
5. Levels also mean increases in revenue and should be considered in all planning and forecasting.

For more information on this topic, go to

www.essentialonlinesolution.com.

Step II

Building Practical, Powerful, Professional Web Sites that WORK

Chapter 5

Understanding Web Sites

The Front Door to Your Online Business

This chapter explains why you want to have a web site and what you need to know before you create one. The focus here is to keep the business and the online initiative aligned and to address the single biggest problem in web site creation: What is the site supposed to do for your prospective customers, the clients you have, and your business? This chapter introduces the terms *desired action, desired results,* and the *One Thing.* It demystifies the myths about web sites and discusses such issues as naming your site and how much information you need to convey.

If you do a Google search on how to create a web site, you will get 1.5 billion results. At first we were thrilled we had so many resources to use; but then we started researching them and it became a journey of countless ideas and ways of approaching the subject. We had to evaluate ideas, philosophies, and techniques against our own personal experiences and the ways in which web sites are most successful. Needless to say, you could write a separate book on just the creation of a web site. This book and our assignment, however, is to focus on the *essentials* of creating a successful web site.

A web site can be the front door to your business, and like the experience you have when you enter the front door of anyone's home, you get an immediate reaction. Sometimes it's beautiful, sometimes it's not. Sometimes it's clean, neat, and organized, while sometimes you can't believe how people could live in a cluttered mess. Your web site can make the first impression someone has of your business. So, this is our first challenge— what kind of impression do you want your web site to give?

But that's wrong! It's not the impression we want to give rather but what the reader wants to read. It's about what the surfer is surfing for. When we conduct seminars with independent business people, we ask them, "How many people have a web site?" We get a near unanimous response that everybody has one. Then we ask, "How many people are pleased with their web site?" Again we get a near unanimous response—not because responders are pleased, but because they are disappointed with the results. Then follow the classic excuses: "We are in the middle of changing the site," "We are going to redo our site," "Our web site isn't finished yet," and so on.

First rule of creating web sites: They are never finished. There are no finish lines. Creating a web site is not a one-time event. It is a process.

First, we look at the myths that need to be put to rest, the absolutes to make that process easier, and the creation of a site that yields results. That is, what you must do or not do in order to be successful online. These are the rules, a new set of beliefs, the dos and don'ts that the majority of web experts agree on for once! These are the *essentials* of building a web site.

THE MYTHS

It's Expensive

Many people believe that building a web site costs thousands of dollars. A custom-designed site could with lots of graphics, hundreds of pages, and all the hours it would take for a web design team to put together. Most successful business sites, however, are simple to create and should cost no more than $100 to produce. We explain how and why it can be done in a later chapter.

It Is a Time-Consuming Process

Wrong! A basic site can be created in a few hours. There are tools available today that speed up the process and actually make it a fun project. Again we will share these sources.

You Have To Be a Nerd

That was true, but now tools are available to create a web site that have made the once required technical expertise...well...obsolete. Software vendors and many web site hosting services provide inexpensive, "user friendly" applications that are easy to use and capable of as much sophistication as you need.

GETTING STARTED

Before you get started building a site, ask yourself these questions:

1. What is the mission of your organization?
2. What is your philosophy of doing business?
3. What will creating a web site do to reinforce your mission?
4. What do you want to accomplish by having a web site?

5. What are your two or three most important goals for the site?
6. Who is your target market primary audience for the web site?
7. What do you want the audience to think or do after visiting your site?
8. How will you adequately maintain the finished site?
9. What web-related strategies will you use to achieve those goals?
10. How will you measure the success of your site?

DEFINING YOUR MARKET

Who is your market? What kind of people are going to be visiting and reading your site? Are they the Mountain Dew generation—young, hip, cool? Do they ride skateboards? Were they raised in a digital world? Are they Baby Boomers approaching 60 in denial, who don't think they're old but need a large enough typeface they can read?

Yes, look at your demographics. Demographics tell us age, income level, occupation, location, and the like. But today it's lifestyle information—psychographics—that is more important. What specialty magazines do your customers read? What television shows do they watch? What kind of car do they drive? The list is endless.

Who you are appealing to should determine the look of your web site—not the "local computer wiz" who sets up web sites. It might be okay. But if the whiz is a kid his or her taste level might be very different from the 40-something you want to shop your site. So ask the question: Does your web site project an appropriate image of your customer?

DESIRED RESULT

Desired result is a key phrase. We define *key phrase* as a universal rule, term, or concept to live by in thinking about web site development and online business—something that is a known or accepted belief.

What is the *desired result* you want from creating and maintaining a web site?

Purpose is one problem that most people have with web development. They don't really understand the purpose of their web site and what they want it to do. If you don't know what you want your site to do, you can't expect potential customers to know for you. Sure, people tell themselves they want to do more business with their web sites. That might be their goal. But how are they going to do more business?

What is the desired result when someone first goes to the home page of your web site? If you just want someone to have a warm fuzzy feeling about your business, is this a desired result? Warm fuzzy feelings are nice, but you are setting your sights too low. Is the site simply informational like a plain telephone listing in the yellow pages? What is the desired result of the look and feel of the site? Is it in alignment with the rest of your marketing and what your company really is? Is it projecting the right image and is it helping to develop your brand?

What do you want the site to do? Do you want to sell products from the site? Do you want the site to be informational, a site that proclaims your business philosophy and tells your story? Do you want to be a resource of information to your customers? Do you want to let prospective clients learn about you and what you can do for them? Is the *desired result* of the site to offer better customer service?

If so, let's look at *Southwest.com.* It may be a large company—but it was founded with the same kind of entrepreneurial spirit that is totally in character with smaller businesses. That is why we will use it as a good example and one that many of you already know no matter where you live.

That said, Southwest Airlines' desired result is to lower the cost of traveling by letting the customers be their own flight reservationists. All airlines do that now—but Southwest increases the level of service because it is letting the customers control their travel plans, even the prices that they pay. The Southwest site is in perfect alignment with the company's philosophy of making things simple.

We single out Southwest because it is one of the easiest airline sites to maneuver. We all know what Southwest wants us to do when we go to its web site. Buy airline tickets.

The bottom line is this: If you don't know what the *desired result* of your web site is, then how is the customer going to know what to make of your web site?

DESIRED ACTION

This is another key phrase.

It is the specific action step you want taken to achieve your desired result. Every page on your web site *must* have a *desired result*. What step or action do you want visitors to take? Which page on the site should they navigate to first? Why should they go there? Should they sign up for your newsletter? If so, how do they do that? Do you want them to buy your products? What will tell them how to make the purchase? Do they click on a button on the left side of the web page? At the bottom? Are the instructions to do so clear? What is the one thing you want them to do on that page?

Do you want your visitors and customers to use telephone or e-mail to contact you for your services? To place orders? Or just to know who you are and what you do or sell so that they will bookmark you for later reference? To use a sports analogy, people want their team to win, but you win with a plan and the right weapons such as a creative offensive scheme, or a time tested defensive strategy and the players to execute them. In short, sports teams and online winners need a game plan. Otherwise you are putting up a billboard inside a deserted alley in a small town off the main highway.

What about the better mousetrap philosophy? If what you sell is so good that the world will seek you out, if you have a product that is different, unique, and unusual, with a believable story and a justifiable price, then word will spread. Google spread —but how many Google ideas are there?

If your idea is so breakthrough, then this book might not be necessary for your success. Nevertheless, even a killer application needs a good web site. There will always be that mystery about something new. Nowadays we know what to expect from Google, what it can do for us, and some of us may even understand how it makes money.

Also, if you are in an industry with lots of competition and the difference in what you and the other guys do is minimal, then keep on reading. You can have 100 different, experienced, qualified electricians wire a house, and almost everyone will end up with the same results. The light switches work.

THE ONE THING

This is like the desired action—however it differs in one major way. *The One Thing's* emphasis is the premise that we only want our pages to accomplish one thing. That is, one page to buy the product, one to take the company tour, one to see the product or the service, one to send referrals. Each page has one assignment, just one desired action. If it has more than one task, it can confuse the reader. The best pages are the simplest.

ALIGNMENT

Now that you have seen the importance of a defined market and identified customers vis-à-vis your future web site, make sure everything you do is in *alignment*. If you say you are known for quality, make sure your site represents quality. If you believe in fast service, make sure your site loads quickly and that its operation and order form are as simple to use for customers as walking into a physical place of business or over the phone. Does your site have the same feel and look of your business? Does your web site project an appropriate image of your company? The web site should reinforce who you are and what you do. What customers experience online should resemble entering a real place of business. It is important because you want instant recognition when someone goes to your site. They won't stay long if your web site does not feel like a real business, your real business, that is. Sure, for the web-only customer it doesn't make any difference because they only know you online. But even they have this expectation that is very human—that there is more behind your web page than just pixels on a screen.

NAMING THE SITE

The first step in developing a site is selecting the domain name. There are many places to register your name, but two of the biggest are *Register.com* and *GoDaddy.com.* GoDaddy is the largest and features the best prices—plus it is always having promotions. Rick bought two new domain names for under $15 for the year. (Understand that is just for the registration of the domain name. It does not include the cost for creating or hosting an active site. In Chapter 7, we go through the steps of creating a web site.)

When you type in the domain name you want at either Register or GoDaddy, you will see if it is available and with what suffix. The suffixes available today are listed at the sites. There are now over 29 different suffixes available. They range from .com, .biz, .net, .org, and on. They are supposed to indicate the type of institution or industry. However, distinctions have faded, say, between a commercial site and an organization site, to allow for these suffixes to be used so that you can use a domain name that has already been taken. For example, if you wanted a .com site and it was not available, you could go with the same domain name but ending it with .net. Of course, .com sites are more desirable for any business. Another option is the newer .biz suffix, but you run the risk of customers and clients inadvertently typing in the .com site.

Godaddy.com and *Register.com* offer other alternatives to select. Just adding words like *the, my, best, original, official*, or *online* before or after a name can secure a name that is still recognizably the one you want. Many people also opt for dashes between words. So instead of *Bobsbarbeque.com*, it would be *bobs-barbeque. com*. The variations you can try are many and still easy to remember and use.

You will also notice that the Internet is an exact science. That means whenever your name is misspelled the traffic will go to the misspelling. Rick Segel is an often misspelled name. Rick's web site is *www.ricksegel.com*. But with Segel spelled in so many different ways Rick also owns *www.ricksegal.com, www.rickseigel.com* and *www.ricksiegel.net*.

Buying up misspelled domain names has become a cottage industry. *Foreclosure.com* made a mistake by not securing *Foreclosures. com.* Just having a competitor add an *s* to a name and securing that web site can hurt your business. It is a small price to pay to secure your name and related possibilities. The thing that is really scary is that there are services available today (GoDaddy offers it) that can purchase a name the second that it expires. That means if you were to forget to renew your domain name, someone could buy it, and then make what was your site into a porno site. How would that affect your business? How much would you pay to get your name back? That depends on how important that site is to you. It's not uncommon for business to pay $5,000, $10,000 or even more to get back hijacked domain names. Of course, you can always take legal action, but the legal charges might not make it worth the effort. But, it is an option. Just make sure you cover all the possibilities so that you don't become a victim of a web opportunist.

The domain name, by the way, doesn't have to have to tell what the business does. *Amazon.com* doesn't exactly convey *onlinebookseller.com.* eBay didn't mean auction when it was first chosen. The issue is, what will people most likely type in the browser when they are looking for you?

Chapter 5's Essential Essentials

1. Get rid of the online myths you have.
2. Define your online marketplace.
3. Know your desired result.
4. Identify what you want the web site to accomplish.

Chapter 5's Essential Essentials, *continued*

5. Know why your customers would do business with you online.

6. Make sure your online business is in alignment with your business's look and feel.

7. Identify what desired actions you want from your-visitors.

8. Understand the pros and cons in domain naming your site.

9. Be conscious of variant spellings and what kind of harm they can do to your business.

10. Focus on why you are creating the site and what it will do for your customer/client, not what it can do for you.

For more information on this topic, go to

www.essentialonlinesolution.com.

Chapter 6

Our Rules for Killer Sites

As we researched this book, we learned things about web sites we liked and did not like. Some web sites confirmed what we accepted or did ourselves. Some web sites had designs that were not widely used but are just gems. This chapter is a collection of impressions and ideas that we converted into our *Basic Rules for Killer Sites*. At first we thought of calling them the Universal Rules to Building Web Sites. But they aren't universal—at least not yet— and they should be. Why? Because it's rare when you see a successful site that doesn't have most of what makes a killer site.

THE THREE P RULES: IT'S THE GOAL

The three Ps sum up everything we are trying to achieve in our online initiatives and web site development. They should always be in our minds when we build our site and maintain it over time.

1. *Pull them in.* This is the attention grabber vistors see first when your web site appears onscreen. It can be a headline, a thought-provoking question, a graphic, or copy that expresses exactly what visitors are looking for.

2. *Prove the point.* Now that you have their attention, prove you are right. Use examples, testimonials, offers, or guarantees.
3. *Purchase.* Show visitors how they can buy, how easy and painless it is, and how safe and secure it is to use your web site.

Convenience Rules

Say *convenience rules* three times and then repeat it every day you have a web site, which should be for the rest of your life. Convenience was the tipping point that made the web the phenomenon that it is today. It isn't price. It is the speed that someone can find exactly what they want. This rule is so important that it has created an entire subcategory of rules. (We refer to the effects of convenience throughout this book because of the far-reaching effects it has on online success.)

The Rule of Specializing

Remember it's all about convenience. You may not need one web site; you may need multiple sites. That is, have a separate site for every business category. You might think that a plumber just does plumbing. However, there are at least three distinct areas in which this kind of business can operate that allow for three smaller sites. A plumber can also host a remodeling site directed to the homeowner who wants to update an old bathroom or even build an addition to his or her house. The second site could be aimed at general contractors who hire subcontractors—in this case, the plumber. (This way, the plumber can end up working on that prospective owner's addition via a different sales stream.) Lastly, the plumber might set up a third site that offers 24-hour emergency maintenance work for those broken pipes.

This hypothetical plumber can have three sites but he or she might want one of these as the primary site that offers all of these services. It will still need to pass the 8-second Rule.

One of the other major advantages to web technology is the speed at which a search engine can find things. That's why the most obscure item sells online. Find your niche and you'll get rich. In retailing it is referred to as "deep and narrow." Pinpointing the product. Just remember, the site doesn't have to be bigger or better. It just has to solve a problem or fill a want for somebody.

The 8-Second Rule: The Match

Studies show us that the web surfer only spends about eight seconds at a web site to determine if it matches up with what they are looking for. That's why those Flash pages can be a waste. While they are still loading the graphics, the prospect is gone. You need to ask what are they searching for and whether your launching page delivers that message as simply and clearly as possible. If not, you lose.

The Rule of Page One: It's All about Customer Benefit

Continuing the 8-Second Rule, the Customer Benefit Page One Rule emphasizes that the first page must be about what the reader is looking for. It's not about us. It's about our prospective client, our customer. What impression will they see? What will this site do for them? What will turn them on and what will it take for them to do what we are asking them to do? It's okay to put your history and how wonderful you are later in the site, just not on page one. This page is for the customer.

Minimum Level of Professionalism Rule

This concept is the anti-*wow* and it is contrary to conventional thinking. For the last 30 years, we have lived by the belief that to succeed, we must be bigger, newer, better, different, unusual, and first to the market. Web sites and successful web businesses are simple and utilitarian. The product might be the *wow*. The photo used could be a *wow,* but the site itself must be uncomplicated, simplistic. Big intros and splash pages are a waste.

The *Minimum Level of Professionalism Rule* states that once you have reached that minimum level of acceptable standards, any money or time you spend will have an insignificant return on the investment. Again, splash pages, those annoying intro pages that always have a button that says *click here to skip*, are a waste of both time and money. Most people skip them. Those pages are done by graphics people, *not* marketing people.

To illustrate my point are two super sites. One of the great success stories on the web is the site *www.bluenile.com*, an online diamond retailer. We can't imagine anyone buying an expensive diamond online; but Blue Nile did over $100 million last year. The site is simple and basic. You don't have to spend extra money for a graphic designer. Just make it simple, easy to use, and logical.

The other successful site is *www.harryanddavid.com*, the gourmet food purveyor. It has the Harry and David company logo, a horizontal and a vertical tool bar, a picture of the product, and a one-paragraph description. There is little scrolling on the site. Every page is a page that fills the window. Graphic designers might hate us, but successful sites have eliminated all of the whiz-bang stuff.

That doesn't mean that these sites aren't clean, neat, crisp, and inviting. They offer that minimum level that people perceive as professional. Understand that different industries have different standards. Bank and investment sites must provide a higher level of professionalism than perhaps the plumber, but not when it comes to ease of use. They are both in the same category.

The Rules of Making the Site Sticky: The Top 10

Roland Lacey of MediaRight Technologies in Massachusetts, one of the first web designers, came up with the concept of a sticky web site. It's one thing getting visitors to your site. But if they leave as quickly as they come, what good is it? So keeping visitors at a site and engaging them to explore further is crucial.

Selecting sticky rule number one wasn't difficult. We believe that copy is king—but we earn our living from writing.

1. *Copy.* Great words paint vivid personal images. The greatest copy line ever written was "Get Rich Quick." Those three words have been so overused and by so many less then reputable people, that it almost has a negative connotation. However, those words are still at the root of many successful ad campaigns. Remember everybody wants to "get" what they want as quickly as possible. It makes sense.

   Killer copy is copy that motivates the reader to act. It is not copy that says you are the greatest thing since sliced bread.

2. *Headlines.* A headline is just the vehicle for great copy. Great copy that the reader skims is wasted. Every paragraph needs a headline. Something that will entice, intrigue, and almost seduce the reader to read further. Copy without a headline is like a day without sun. Gray and boring.

3. *Pictures.* After reviewing many sites, we are convinced that the sites that look the most professional have the best photographs. We can look at sites and comment on how beautiful they are and then realize it's not the site, it is pictures of what they sell and the benefits of what they sell.

A professional speaker, for example, does this with a photograph of a laughing or smiling audience.

Some of the best web sites consist of navigation bars, photographs, and simple but effective short copy with clear and bold headlines.

4. *Graphic Design*. The graphic treatments are comprised of the following items:

   • Backgrounds
   • Colors and color themes (also called your trade dressing)
   • Symbols, icons, trademarks, and logos
   • Fonts that project the look a "company likes to keep"
   • Highlighting, white space, capital lettering, italicizing, and framing text and images

   These are all graphical treatments that create that sticky feel.

5. *Offers*. The Godfather made an offer they couldn't refuse. Do the same (just don't be so violent). Make the offer a real *wow*. Something that will get people talking about you. A trial period, no risk offer, a lost leader price or the ultimate of all offers, it's *free!*

6. *Free*. What can you give away that has value to your prospect? This has become the most proven technique used online today—especially when it just needs to be free information. Google built an empire by providing its search engine for free. Banks offer free mortgage calculators. Many businesses offer free newsletters. Office furniture companies offer free office space planning. Credit bureaus offer free credit reports.

   Every business should offer some kind of free information. Why? It positions you as an expert—and we like to do business with the experts.

7. *Tips*. One of the best tools that make a reader stick around your site is the free weekly or monthly tip. These are short tidbits of information that have value and create community. The tip itself or an e-mail sign-up can be placed inside a text box or even a discrete and unobtrusive popup. We recommend the use of a tastefully done popup screen that is 2 × 4 inches in size inviting visitors to sign up for a free tip service. We will receive criticism because many people believe the popup screen was made by the devil and is an intrusion of privacy.

    WE agree, however, the type of popup that is on your own site, that is enhancing the visitors' experience, is not an invasion of anyone's privacy.

    The bigger issue is that difference in tip sign-ups is 9 to 1. Nine more people will sign up with the popup than without it. This type of popup does not deserve the bad reputation that most popups have.

8. *Tours*. Offer a free tour of your site and what it can do for you. You can use a PowerPoint presentation highlighting the benefits of your site to the reader—or a Flash movie—that the visitor can choose to see.

9. *Lessons*. Offer free classes at the site or via e-mail. The "classes" should consist of three to four short lessons separated by a few days for greater impact.

10. *Testimonials, Testimonials, Testimonials*. These motivate people to buy. The more believable they are, the higher the sales. Testimonials belong on more than just a testimonial page. We are not against having one—just that they are rarely viewed as such. Instead, have them placed throughout your site. Think in terms of context. If you have a service that solves a problem, then have testi-

monials that show how you solved it and exceeded your clients' expectations.

One of the technologies that will become a mainstay is the use of the talking testimonials. These are either a photograph of the person with an audio clip playing or an actual video clip with someone praising the company and their experience. These clips should last less than a minute. Many times the testimonial will answer many of the questions a prospect might already have.

11. *Audio and Video Clips*. Use multimedia technology to add audio and video clips to quote your clients' testimonials when they praise your service or product. These clips can be a photograph and an audio clip or a short movie lasting less then a minute. You can also welcome people to the site with audio and video, telling them what your company is all about, how it benefits others, and the best way to use the site.

Many people find it easier to talk than write about what they do, and a talking testimonial can add a personalized flavor to the many times impersonal world of technology.

There are many more ideas that make a site sticky. We wanted to give you the top 10—plus a bonus one. And some ideas didn't make the list but should also be mentioned. The autoresponder, for example, instantly sends an e-mail is the sign of a well run professional business. It acknowledges us instantly. It thanks us for our purchases.

One other sticky element belongs in the top 10. We struggled over including it. This is the freshness rule—keeping the site fresh with new pictures, testimonials, and material. Why didn't it make it top the top 10 list? Because this only applies to repeat customers or readers. The first timer doesn't know that you have used the same quote for five years. It is still very important to keep the site fresh.

THE RULE OF STATS: READ THEM AND USE THEM

How good is your site?

Your site is finished. It is registered with the search engines. It is up and running. How do you determine how well it's working and what steps you need to take to make it a success? Almost every web-hosting company provides a service that reports the site's performance. It collects information such as how many unique visitors come to your site, how long they stay, what page they see first (not everyone uses the front door), and what page, more than any other, people use to exit your site. It also collects information on what pages are the most popular and what headlines and pictures work the best.

Statistics can answer other questions as well. There may be 50 ways to leave your lover, but how many ways to leave your site? Are there any sections that are more powerful than others? How many visitors return to your site, and what do they return for? Are there some pages no one visits? Knowing this information can help you make changes to your web site to improve its performance.

What's the point? Most people don't review their performance reports as we have discovered. They don't understand that sites need to be tweaked. Sometimes it is a simple headline that can change the performance of a page. It might just be a picture that is not getting your message across.

The most important stat is the *conversion rate.* That is, how many people visit a site in relationship to how many people purchase something—for example, how many people buy per every 100 visitors. There are other conversion rates such as how many people sign up for a tour, a free class, or subscribe to a newsletter.

As Ken Evoy of Site Sell says, "It's not about building a site, it's about building a business." After all spending, the time to develop a site and then only complaining that the site isn't working is foolish. Yes, the ultimate test is whether or not your sales are improving. Reading the statistics supplied by your site or purchasing an additional service from an outside vendor that monitors this information can be the most valuable information you will ever learn about your business. It is your own personalized market research, and this market research doesn't lie.

Chapter 6's Essential Essentials

1. Killer sites have many similarities.
2. The Ps to Profit are Pull them in, Prove the point, and Purchase. It's the same as buy low and sell high. It's an easy concept to understand but hard to master.
3. Convenience—it's the tipping point of the web. Make it easy to understand and use.
4. 8-Second Rule—web surfers must discover a match within the first eight seconds of landing on your page or they are gone.
5. The First Page Rule—as important as the 8-Second Rule, this rule states that the first page had better express what the visitor is looking for.

Chapter 6's Essential Essentials, *continued*

6. Minimum Level of Professionalism—it's the contra-*wow*, where there is no significant return on your investment beyond a certain level of professionalism. Flash introductions can waste time and what you spend on them doesn't equate more success.

7. Specialize, have multiple sites that express the different specializations of your business. People search for specialists. Treat yourself as one.

8. Sticky—use the sticky rule ideas for copy, headlines, pictures, free and the like.

9. Read your statistics. They tell you who goes to your site and how long they stay, and help you to focus on why they leave.

For more information on this topic, go to

www.essentialonlinesolution.com.

Chapter 7

Building Your Web Site

It's Easier than You Think

This chapter discusses the essentials of building a web site from layout, design, and templates to the value of web designers and webmasters. Then we break down all the possible navigation options and elements that go into a web site. The chapter concludes with a step-by-step guide to building your web site, whether you are building it yourself or someone else is helping you. It will give you the knowledge to make informed—and profitable—decisions.

UNDERSTANDABLE LAYOUTS: CLUTTER KILLS

People hate following directions that are complicated. Word everything at your web site simply—just like your newspaper, which is written at a fifth grade level. Make it simple, such as *Click Here to Sign Up for Our Newsletter,* or *Learn More About* _____ or *Get Involved in our Once in a Lifetime Opportunity.* The same principle applies to any instructions where your visitor must click to read what your business does or where to read a case study or testimonial page. Many sites will actually list the steps 1–2–3 as if talking to a child. It's okay. People appreciate that level of simplification. After all, isn't that what "user friendly" means? Remember, it's all about convenience.

Navigation Bars: The SAAB Effect

Have you ever driven a Saab automobile? For most of the Saab line, the first experience many usually have in a Saab driver's seat is figuring out where the key goes. It is not on the steering column or near the dashboard. It's in the center console between the two front seats. It's different—and you have to get used to it.

That is the same feeling you get when you go to a web site that you have never visited before, when you can't find the navigation bar buttons. We have become accustomed to having the navigation bars in certain places. Having a navigation bar on the right side of the page throws people off unless it is clearly marked, and even that is an uncomfortable feeling.

In our quest to be different and stand out in a crowd, we will sacrifice instant usability. The site must be logical. Readers need to know where to go instinctively. When a page is too cluttered, it can confuse people and they will get lost. A designing "no-no" is having a layout with four columns of data. It just doesn't work. Three columns work with the middle column being the heart of the page and the two side columns consisting of links to other pages, features, and content. Be careful not to offer too many options for people to choose.

Our point here is to select a site layout that offers a level of familiarity so that a visitor stays. We might take the time to find where the key goes in a Saab—but we won't wait eight seconds on your site if it is a mess.

Headlines

The one other tip to better layouts is the effective use of headlines. Sometimes all vistors read are the headlines—so don't clutter things up with too much copy.

TO TEMPLATE OR NOT TO TEMPLATE

Should you pay someone to design and create a new and a personalized web site just for you? This just doesn't make sense to us. For many kinds of business sites, the need for a web designer is not as important as it once was. (There is still a need for someone to layout what is needed to make the site work. Maybe the new title should be the web planner.)

Instead, use a template—that is, a predesigned style and format. These are offered for sale by literally thousands of sources online—and by the web-hosting and site-creation companies such as GoDaddy, Yahoo!, or *Register.com*.

Why?

First, why spend the money? Second, most templates allow you to customize and add special treatments—that and your own content, pictures, and preferences for fonts and the like make the difference. If you are afraid of looking like your competition or if another business comes along and does what you do, don't worry. A few years ago those problems existed because there were few templates available. Today there are thousands available from many different sources. We have seen one template used by hundreds of businesses and none of the resulting web sites look exactly alike. It is just a plain white background with a simple navigation bar.

The best analogy we can give is that favorite color in practically every mall: beige. Most people go to the mall and never notice it. It's a neutral color. Customers' eyes focus on the message instead—not the wall.

WHAT'S IN THE SITE?

What should go into a web site has an infinite amount of answers. It all goes back to what do you want your web site to do and who your target market is. How many sections should a web site have? Of course, the fewer the sections and subcategories, the less confusing or intimidating the site becomes. In the following list—based on actual web sites that we have researched—and the most important sections, the ones that are hard to live without. You do not need all of these categories as main sections, either. Some can be subsections, accessed by a pull-down menu.

Before we address the issue of categories we must look at a style of site that doesn't have any navigation buttons or tabs at all. It is a straight sales letter that will go on for 15 to 20 pages. Within that sales letter there might be some audio or video testimonials but there aren't any traditional types of categories or sections. It is a straight sales letter whose purpose in life is to sell you, or have you sample a product or service.

These sections are the possible navigation buttons or tabs. Have fun picking what is important to you, but especially to your customer.

- *The Home Page.* This should be the attention grabber. The page that matches the visitor's wants or needs. It is the page that will lure them into the site. We call this page the *benefit page* to the visitor and it is one of the key elements that make a site work. The goal is to create a feeling of confidence—that the prospect has come to the right spot. Your site must fulfill that feeling. People don't just buy grass seed, they are buying a beautiful lawn.

- *About Us.* This tells about the business, what it does, who it serves, the history, the employees, and the ownership. The mission could be included here as a subsection. There could be a number of subsections from this tab such as Services, People, Mission, Philosophy, and so on.

- *Services.* This category tells what you do. It lists your capabilities and specialties.

- *Our People.* This section focuses on your employees. In many businesses, this is their greatest asset and their biggest differentiator—their people. If that is the case, make "Our People" one of your major tabs on the site. Show pictures of them, length of employment, and a brief description about family or values. Take a group picture and explain what the people in the photograph can do for you.

- *Mission.* Most businesses have a mission statement that its personnel live by. There are businesses that have a strong signature line or advertising slogan. This is the place to put it and the place to tell the world why you do what you do.

- *Vision Statement.* A vision statement gives an insight to the purpose and future of the company—where you see the company growing in the next 10–15–20 years. This is a category that could easily be a subsection of About Us.

- *Tour.* This has become a very popular tab with more aggressive online marketers. It is a soft sell that will take the reader through a process of defining a problem, explaining typical remedies, and how your business can become the solution. This is sometimes done through a PowerPoint type presentation with audio highlighting the various stops on the site. It always ends with a Desired Action of signing up for a free trial, purchasing, or just a way to opt in to a newsletter or e-mail advertisements.

- *Trial.* The free trial offer is still one of the most effective ways to make a long-time relationship. Many people feel it is so important that they give it a separate tab. We believe this can be accomplished with a box or button link rather than as a separate category; but many businesses believe it should have both options.

- *Other Links.* This can be a powerful tab because the very best source for generating web business comes from referrals from other businesses. It is the number one traffic generator for a site and should not be taken lightly. Having *Other Links* as a navigation tab can also mean that you are thanking other business for their referrals to you. However, it can also be used as a profit center by creating a page of referrals that you have an affiliate or associate program with. This means if someone goes to the site and purchases something you receive a commission. However, *don't* just do this for the commission. Make sure it is a resource you would normally recommend. (Linking will be covered more in other chapters.)

- *Partners.* This is another way of saying links. The same rules apply.

- *Contact Us.* This is required to do business. It can include an e-mail address as well as your physical location address, telephone, and fax.

- *Awards and Testimonials.* We differ with many businesses about this section. Customers rarely view this page because they see it as "fluff." Yet a good testimonial or winning a major industry award can catapult a business to new levels. Our recommendation is that testimonials and awards should be positioned throughout your site in context.

- *Locations.* A navigation button for locations is used when a business has multiple physical locations. Every major retailer will have this as a key navigation feature. They also include a map, a link to Google, or MapQuest for a map and directions.
- *Products/Services.* If you sell from your site, make sure one of your navigation buttons clicks to your products or services. Customers should not have to search very hard for this button or tab! If there is more than one kind of product or service, allow for access to subsections. This section should have a *Checkout* button to start the transaction process.
- *New Products.* This is used when you have a new release or if you are known for new and different products all of the time. Anytime you want to highlight a product launch, make sure you have this navigation button.
- *In the News.* This section is where to present any press or media clips your company receives.
- *Contests.* A contest section is important for those businesses that use contests to build their business. A framed text box is also an option for this feature as well as a permanent navigation spot.
- *Our Ads.* This is an overlooked category. But if you are a business with constant circulars or multiple or different ads, then this should become a key section.
- *Frequently Asked Questions (FAQs).* Clients and prospects appreciate when it is easy to find answers to common questions that are short and understandable.
- *Event Info.* If your business plans seminars, meetings, or trade shows, this is a critical section.

- *Policies.* Legal notices, copyright statements, and similar warnings go on this page. You can have a separate section or just include it as a subcategory of your mission or vision statement.
- *Check Out.* Without this you are building a store without a cash register. This MUST be the easiest and simplest of them all. Never have them hunt for this tab.
- *Articles.* Your web site can be the perfect storage facility for your newsletters and articles. Articles will help grow the site and make the web site come up more often on search engines. Depending on your business, this can be the fast lane to gaining expertise status.
- *Links.* A link can also be to specific, related points of interest about your business such as a blog or auction items on eBay. These types of links differ from other links that refer people to unrelated sites.
- *Feedback.* Some businesses find that a feedback button is important even though few people use it. If you need to limit yourself, this one doesn't make the cut.
- *Site Map.* Site maps are important when web sites consist of pages and pages of information. There are services available that will do this for you.
- *Job Openings.* This is a critical section. Young people don't go to the local McDonald's site for the ingredients or the current price of a Happy Meal. They go to check out the job openings.
- *Catalogs.* For some businesses, catalog pages and/or downloadable catalog documents are how they market their products. You may need a techie to get this functionality.
- *Calendar of Events.* This section can be used for advertising sales and promotional events and other kinds of schedule tracking to generate business or manage it (such as dis-

playing when you are booked, on vacation, or seasonal). A contractor or consultant might use it for booked dates, and another business might use it as a fun section for the off-beat and unusual happenings in its business.

TOOLS AND ELEMENTS FOR YOUR SITE

There are a number of techniques that increase the effectiveness of a web site. Do you need them all? *No.* Think of this section as a menu from which to choose tips and tools. Like good servers at a fine restaurant, we will editorialize a bit and share our favorites and must-dos.

- *Autoresponder.* Technically this is not part of your web site. But if you are asking for information from a prospect or customer, even just an e-mail address, you want your site to automatically send an e-mail thanking them. Needless to say, such thank-you notes, order confirmations, and the like are just common courtesy and good business.
- *Audio Feeds.* Due to the increase in bandwidths and more people using cable modems rather than dial-up, audio and video messages have become more popular. There are many companies that supply this technology and it is inexpensive.

  This method can be highly effective because you deliver your message in your own voice. One way it works is to have a picture of yourself with a play button under it.
- *Video Feeds.* Our feeling is to stick with audio. Video is fine, but the quality can be less than perfect, not because of the technology, but because you run the risk of looking amateurish. Lighting and speaking into a camera require expertise and time to master. It might look easy, but to be effective you need experience.

- *Surveys, Evaluations, Assessments, and Tests.* Companies exist that offer inexpensive and even no-fee surveys, tests, and other kinds of evaluations that you can customize and put on your web site. These can be nice features because they add value and keep people coming back. Rick's site has a "Retail Store Assessment" for his retail clients. The variations are endless. Our plumber example could sponsor a test on the 10 Ways to Check If You Need a New Hot Water Heater. As you can see, this is a presale tool and a way to qualify a customer.

  Make the tests honest and above-board. If you try to manipulate the answers, it will hurt you in the end.

- *Signed Message from Owner.* This technique adds a personal touch to a web site. Make it brief—you could share the reason why you are in business and what it means to you. This will personalize your company's mission statement. It's the touch that gives that warm, fuzzy feeling.

- *Associate and Affiliate Programs.* Referring business from one web site to another is rapidly gaining acceptance and becoming an industry by itself. If a sale results from the referral, it earns a commission. This practice is increasing in popularity because almost anyone selling online can offer such a program. That is why you are seeing more and more referral sites popping up. These are sites whose sole purpose is to refer business to other sites. We now recommend this service, even when it may not result in a direct sale, because it still provides a service to customers—they still get something they need from your site and you still can profit. Just ask yourself this question, "What else does the customer need if they are coming to my site?"

- *Private Sections.* Unlike the free side of the web site, which might offer a free test or information, the private section is accessed by those willing to pay a subscription or fee. Here there are more offerings, such as a detailed report. This can be a real money maker.

- *Shop Online, Pick Up at Business.* The goal of any web business is to integrate the bricks and the clicks. The online-side order and the physical location pickup can make for a seamless customer experience of your business rather than keeping the two sides separate. Isn't that the way it should be?

- *RSS Feeds.* Really Simple Syndication—RSS—was designed for sharing news without sending it via e-mail. RSS provides the latest information downloads to users' computers. Think of it as a distributable "What's New" for your site. Originated by UserLand in 1997, creating your own RSS feed or subscribing to one that provides news relevant to your business can be a focal point on your web site and a reason for visitors to keep coming back. RSS feeds are a solution to the myriad problems webmasters commonly face, such as spam filters that block your e-mail newsletters from reaching your subscribers, and gathering and distributing news. Using RSS feeds is important because it is a way of bypassing e-mail blockers and getting your messages directly to the people who want to read them. This is becoming a must-have box on anyone's web site that produces newsletters or information to share.

BUILDING THE SITE

Step One: Do It Yourself or Hire a Pro? What You Need to Know

The purpose of this book is to show you how easy and inexpensive it is to create an online business. That doesn't mean you have to do it yourself. It simply means being an educated consumer. Sure, you may need an outside consultant for some features of your site. However, a web site is not the mystery many people think it is. It is important to understand the process of creating and maintaining one—after all, you can and should have the skills to make simple changes on your site without waiting for someone else to do them—and charge you for it.

We have always disliked the words "do it yourself." In fact, we rarely do anything ourselves. But when it comes to creating a web site, we advocate doing much of the work yourself because many of the web-hosting services walk you through the entire process. Their customer service is that good and very helpful.

You might wonder why a company would hand-hold for something that doesn't cost that much. Estimated costs for some sites are less than $20 to get started. It is because of the lifetime value that their customers have, which can be significant.

The choice of you building your own site or letting a web designer/developer do it is yours. Like anything else you do, the first time is intimidating. But the more involved you become the easier the process becomes. If you decide to let someone else create your web site, you should read on and understand the process and get more value from whoever does the work.

Step Two: Pick Your Pages—Site Sections and Navigation

We thought of making this step about site layout or planning. That, however, would force you down a path of too much decision making. So we approached this same page with another, simpler way. We recommend selecting the seven most important sections from our master list, the seven you see as having navigation tabs or buttons. For now, we have done that for you and have even added some recommended subsections as well.

- *Home.* This first page *must* answer visitors' needs. There must be a match. What is the biggest benefit you offer your customer?

- *About Us.* It could have on one page or in subsections:
  - Company History
  - Message from the President
  - Business Philosophy
  - Our People
  - Guarantees & Policies
- *Services.* This section should address:
  - What do you do? Or what you sell?
  - How do you do it that's different than your competitors?
  - Why should they do business with you?
  - Who is your customer?
- *Free Tips.* This can be a sign-up for a tip list, a newsletter, or just a place where there are free articles. This is the place to position you as the expert.

    This could also offer a free tour or mini-class of interest to the reader.

  - *Contact Us.*
  - *Locations.* This section can function as a *Contact Us* page, too. It is also a good place for a map.
  - *Links.* What other sites would benefit your visitor? These sites can be part of an affiliate programs. Just make sure you would recommend them, even without the commission.
  - *How to Buy.* If you sell merchandise, this page should work as a shopping cart. If you are selling a service, this page must be a path to the next step in the process of obtaining your services. This section converts the visitor into a buyer. The process can also entail a follow-up call, sending some information via snail mail or an e-mail or a series of e-mails, a face-to-face meeting, or even follow up with personal contact.

These are just hypothetical examples covering the widest group of businesses. But by going though this process you create a plan, a layout in your mind, and, most important, it forces you to examine why you are doing this at all.

Step Three: Select a Web Site Company and Decide What Kind of Business You Want to Do with It

Thousands of companies can help you create a web site. The biggest and least expensive is *GoDaddy.com*. Others include *Yahoo.com, Register.com, Interland.com, SiteBuilder.com,* and *Imac.com* to name some major players. However, there are thousands of other companies jumping on board with great offerings—large companies such as eBay and Microsoft, and many small firms as well. We have selected GoDaddy not because it is the best, but because it is the biggest, most economical, a household name (advertising on the Super Bowl doesn't hurt) and it offers all of the services a small business could need to get started. There are other services we might prefer, but GoDaddy has excellent 24/7 customer service and is a good place to start an online business.

Let's first understand what GoDaddy can do for you:

1. Help select a domain name. This is a free service.
2. Register the name you select. The annual fees range from $1.95 to $40 depending on the suffix you choose (.info sites are in the $1.95 range).
3. Parking. This is where the domain name is securely stored. You don't want a fly-by-night webmaster in charge of parking your name so that you control it.
4. Registering. When the site is created, GoDaddy, like other companies like it, register your site with all of the major search engines.

5. Hosting. Here GoDaddy actually stores your web site on its server.

Another resource we would like to mention is *www.register.com*. It does everything that GoDaddy does, but also offers a service where it will create the site for you. It's a little more expensive than GoDaddy, but if you don't want to take the time to do it yourself, it's a good alternative.

Step Four: Select a Name

When selecting a name, you do not have to use the name of what you are selling. After all, eBay and Amazon are pretty successful and they don't say online *auction.com* or *bookseller.com*. Just make the name distinctive and easy to remember.

Step Five: Select a Template

A template is the way the site's web pages are formatted with your special look. Are you going to have two columns on either side of the page? Are you going to have text boxes? How will the style change per page?

The most common layouts have the navigation bar to the left of the page. (That does not mean it is the only correct place to put a navigation bar. It is just the most common.) We also prefer a column down the right side for testimonials and announcements. Experiment with the various templates to make sure they will achieve your desired result.

Selecting a template from a web service does *not* mean you are selecting colors, style, or finished product. Nevertheless, some companies are more rigid than others. Call the company's toll-free number before you pay for their services to make sure you can get the colors and styles you want. Most companies are flexible today, and this is generally not a problem. However, if a company is too rigid for your tastes, then switch.

Step Six: Select a Style

Selecting a template may mean selecting colors, fonts, and other style features. But we have broken this process into another step. When you talk about style, you are talking about three elements that define you and your site. They are:

1. *Color.* This is referred to as your *trade dressing*. What colors do you use in your business and what colors do you want to be associated with? Caution on colors. Don't focus on wild colors, focus on the content. Whatever colors you pick, make sure the page is readable. Sites with purple pages and red lettering are simply not readable. Before you go helter skelter in selecting your colors, let me remind you that some of the most profitable sites use only a white background.

2. *Fonts.* Fonts can subtly set a mood, create a feeling, an attitude, a sense of professionalism—or a feeling of fun and whimsy. Select fonts wisely, but make sure they are readable and big enough for the baby boom generation turning 60 in the next few years.

3. *Pictures.* This is what makes a site come alive. When we researched and reviewed business web sites, we liked the ones with the best photographs. If you use stock images, make sure they have good pixel resolution and clarity, and that they add value to your web site—not wreck it. There are more pictures available today on the web that can work wonders to your site. Choose pictures wisely and see how they look online before you fall in love with them.

Step Seven: Enter Your Copy

Pictures make the site come alive—but great copy sells goods and services. Here are just two tips that will increase the readability of your site. First, headlines and keywords are what people read. They don't read long paragraphs of copy. They want the bullet points. It makes it easy to read. A keyword or phrase is something in the paragraph that you either highlight, *italicize*, **bold**, CAPITALIZE, or *ALL OF THE ELEMENTS*.

Just doing that alone will have a significant difference. To make your copy even more powerful, use this tip most of all—what we call the Copywriter's Creed: *Write every word for the benefit of the reader, not you.* Don't tell people how great you are. Tell them why they will benefit from doing business with you.

Step Eight: Adding E-commerce—The Shopping Cart

This is one of the most daunting parts of building a commercial web site. But it does not have to be. *Amazon.com* created a wonderful—and now universally accepted—model to follow for displaying products and processing sales online. It is the world's accepted model; it's the way the world likes to buy online. Why are we trying to reinvent the process?

The lessons from Amazon for us to model:

1. Allow your items to be searched in multiple ways: price, style, look, advantages, manufacturer, and producer.
2. Have a small picture of product with short enticing caption that will make you click the picture for a more detailed description.
3. Once clicked, you get a more in-depth description or sales pitch. You also see readers' reviews, what books have been viewed, what books have been purchased with this one, a sample chapter, a bundling opportunities with another items, rankings, a story about the book or author—all this copy *sells*! Everything described involves selling tactics constructed to service the needs of customers and influ-

ence them to buy. And this is the way to sell today and the way people want to buy. We should all adopt it.

4. They track our tastes and recommend items in the future.
5. The checkout process couldn't be any easier. Amazon even features an express checkout system that stores customer information. You can check out in less than one minute.

The bottom line is the way Amazon blends information in a short and long form with great sales techniques, speed, and matchless efficiency in the order processes. Copy Amazon—it is the standard bearer.

Step Nine: Test, Test, Test

Too many people miss the test, test, test step when their site is "finished" but not ready to go live. Start testing; seek opinions from friends, family, and business associates. Tell them to be honest and to compare your site to other sites. Check the loading speed of every page. Make sure all of your links work. Go to an independent web evaluation service such as *Webmechanic.com*, which technically checks your site. The most important aspect is that your site is logical, with its navigation features achieving your *desired action,* and in alignment with your *desired result*.

Step Ten: Publish Your Site

When your finished web site is uploaded—that is, saved—on your Web host's server, which is connected to the Internet and the World Wide Web, it is officially published. You then pay a fee for the web hosting. What you also get, in addition to Internet exposure, is this: Your site can be accessed and registered with Google, Yahoo! and other search engine services.

Again there are plenty of companies willing to host your site. *GoDaddy.com* and other companies that help you build your site also host and register it. Before you get carried away with the companies that tell you they are going to submit your site to hundreds of search engines, if you registered with just Google, MSN, and Yahoo!, you can do just fine. That does *not* mean that you shouldn't submit to the other search engine services. It just means that they are much less important than many of services would have you believe.

Step Eleven: Track Your Visitors

You are up and running. Now it is time to start checking to see where your visitors come from, which search engines they use, what page they enter first, what headlines they respond to and which ones turn them off, and from what page they leave your site.

Now you are ready to start to promote your site!

Chapter 7's Essential Essentials

1. Eliminate clutter from your site—eliminate choices.
2. Learn the killer designs you can use in your web site.
3. Create simple layouts.
4. Web designers and webmasters—what roles do they play and who do you need?
5. Templates and styles—know the difference.
6. What kinds of pages and navigation should there be?
7. What seven categories are you selecting and why?
8. The Saab effect affects us all. How does it affect you?
9. Map and plan your steps to web site creation.
10. What are the other elements that you can add to your site without getting too cluttered?

For more information on this topic, go to

www.essentialonlinesolution.com.

Chapter 8

The Winners and Losers

Web Site Critiques of the Good, the Bad, and the Ugly

I t only takes a moment to know if you like a web site and will stay to buy. This chapter teaches you those subtle things that make a web site work.

OUR METHOD OF RATING

We thought the easiest way for us to understand what makes a great web site was to look at a lot of them. With few exceptions, we won't mention the names of sites that we found negative. We will mention those that deserve kudos.

What we looked for are characteristics that jumped out, stood out. It might be good or bad copy. It might be navigation, color, or a whole variety of different items. But the common denominator is: Be it good or bad, it sticks out.

Even in the most successful online businesses, you can pick out glaring errors in a web site. Conversely, in some marginal or poor sites, there are some winning elements. The issue that we have debated over is whether to use examples from large business with substantial resources. Barbara believed our examples should only be from small businesses. Rick felt we could learn from the sites of large businesses provided that we did not recommend things that are very costly. The bottom line is you will see both large and small sites represented.

Web Essential 1

Don't get hung up on whiz-bang technology. Make your site convenient and user friendly.

Losing Element Site

The first site that we will not mention by name is in the service area. It was created by a contractor who has done a magnificent job with Google's pay-per-click program. He comes up on the top of the sponsor list in almost every search that you do for his category in the region. His copy to get you to click is terrific. He also comes up very high in organic search engine optimization. So what makes this a loser site? When you click the site, you get a message that says, "To enter the site you must use a Flash 5 plug-in and have a screen resolution of 800 × 600 for proper viewing." How many people know what a Flash 5 plugin is, and do they care? Bottom line, we couldn't get into the site. All that advertising was for nothing.

Web Essential 2

Break your offering down into logical chunks of information. Also take your customer's age into account when planning the readability of your site.

Winning Element Site

Harry & David's web site—*http://www.harryanddavid.com*—has winning online elements. Okay, it is not a small business, but we can learn from its site. We believe this is a must-see site for any online entrepreneur because of its simplicity and the way it captures the essence of what online shopping is all about. When you first look at this site, there is a *wow*. It looks great. When you break it down, you realize that the site has a white background, black text, highlights in red—and the most important thing is the page is not very deep so there is no or very little scrolling down. The site has two basic navigation bars, one on the top and one on the side. It also has first-class photographs of the merchandise being sold with a short caption. Because of the logical layout and navigation, you don't get confused by the choices.

Web Essential 3

Don't focus on the price as first thing. Let them fall in love with what you do first. And then let's worry about the price. Can you imagine walking into a retail landscaping store and having the door opened by an employee who says to you: "We have financing available"?

Losing Element Site

We'll now look at a landscape contractor site. When you enter the site on the home page, the first words you see are "Financing available." Is the business doing this on purpose to turn people away? Why would you stay? We left.

Web Essential 4

Personalize your site in every way you can.

Winning Element Site

A ten-year-old online and mail order catalog merchant that does over $10 million a year is Junonia at *www.junonia.com*. This site was one of the winners of Internet Retailers Best of the Web for 2005. The reason why we like it is because of the personalization of the president, Anne Kelly. There's a homey, folksy picture of her holding her dog as she welcomes you into the site right on the front page. Her handwritten signature also gives a personal feel. This site has a section on the home page that is *What Customers Say about Junonia Active Apparel.* It's a testimonial; but it's integrated into the site as opposed to having a separate page. *Junonia.com* does have a separate page called *Community Forum* that is a wonderful collection of articles, interviews, testimonials, partners, links, and the company story. And, unlike the average web site, that says "Contact us," this page features a box to "Contact Anne Kelly," again with her picture. The only negative—a minor point—is the term *community*. Does that reflect all the wonderful things in this page?

Web Essential 5

High ranking on Google can kill you if you have a web site that undermines your standing. This person's web site is so unprofessionally done that it hurts him rather than helps him.

Losing Element Site

In doing a search for accountants in a metropolitan area, we found an accounting firm—named for its owner—that resulted from a Google search at position number 6 from 1.7 million possibilities. This is not bad—until you enter the site. It would be a Level One site. No real background about the individual and definitely not an easy site to navigate. It was almost deceptive because a navigation tab says *Client Letters*, which we would assume to be testimonial letters. Not here. We found he has a downloadable .PDF document of trust income and the like. Where are the client letters? Also he does not have his address on the web site but does list the phone number and an e-mail link. The worst part is his home page, which states he is a member of various organizations, including the American Institute of Certified Public Accountants—but under it, in parentheses, it reads "former member." How stupid can you be? Enough said.

Web Essential 6
Make technology work for your customers to make buying online easy. Period.

Winning Element Site
How many times have you been stumped about what to buy someone? That's the reason we choose *Findgift.com* at *www.findgift.com/ Gift-Shops*. This site is a winner. This site makes gift buying easy. It has a *Gift Wizard* that leads you to some great gifts for that special person or occasion. This site scours the web to provide the shopper with gifts ideas. It's an online mall. You get to select different stores. It's a trend to be aware of—*referral sites*. We will cover these when we discuss affiliates.

Web Essential 7
If you can't get to Level One of online commerce then don't do it.

Losing Element Site
This insurance agent's web site is a first-generation web site. It is a single page with just contact information and an uncomplimentary picture of an ugly building. It gets better. You are invited to visit the insurance agent's hometown. Obviously, this is a community effort to put businesses on the web with a placeholder site. To keep a site looking like this does more harm than good. (Earlier we mentioned the Saab effect, making sure your site has

understandable navigation. A placeholder site from a chamber or association is different from that type of site because a place-holder site from a chamber or association is simply a site that looks the same as your neighbor's site. The only element that changes is the name of the site.)

Web Essentials 8

Take advantage of your assets. Have separate web sites for separate businesses. Accept charge cards—otherwise, you are not in business. Make the site easy to read and include subject headlines.

Winning Element Site (but with a Losing Element)

We reviewed as many different sites in as many different industries as possible. So when it came time to look at real estate sites, we automatically went to the site of one of the most successful real estate brokers in New England, Nelson Zide of ERA Key Reality, Natick, MA—*www.nelsonzide.com*. Our issue is not that the site doesn't have what it needs. It is the fact that it is difficult to find the things that make Nelson Zide and Key Realty an industry leader. Nelson Zide is a published author, regular trainer, and a dynamic speaker who is also a leading salesperson and realty owner. When you go to his site, you don't see that. The other issue is that he has a wealth of information under a simple heading, *Buying and Selling Tips*. In the *About Me* page he doesn't use head-lines or bold typefaces to make the content stand out. On his home page, he has a boxed link that says *Products to Purchase*. Does that really sound compelling enough to make someone purchase his how-to-sell real estate books, audio CDs, and tapes? And there are no pictures of these items. Finally, he does not accept credit cards, which makes it less convenient to buy his products.

Web Essentials 9

Use pleasing colors, section off information, and a make logical and professional presentation. This is the strongest argument for a professionally designed site.

Winning Element Site

SusanBaker.com—www.susanbaker.com—is a site we liked very much. First, the site has the element of a personal welcome on the upper left corner of the home page. Susan Baker is a health care speaker and her superb headline is *Speaking of Exceptional Patient Care*. Her web site has seven navigation tabs on the top. Each tab describes exactly where you will go when you click it. That shouldn't be a *wow,* but after reviewing so many web sites, it's refreshing to see the same headings at the top of the page. *Meet Susan* opens *Meet Susan,* and so on. On the left side of the screen, you have tips sheets, quick ideas for everyday challenges, which is visitor focused. In the same column, the site features where to sign up for Susan Baker's quarterly newsletter. In the middle of the page is a testimonial using large quotation marks for graphical emphasis. As well as the navigation tabs, there are links in the middle of the page that access three of the main sections of the site. There is also a photograph of Susan Baker, descriptions of her and her services, and links to Barnes & Noble for her best selling book, *Managing Patient Expectations.* The thing that is so impressive about the home page is that even with so much information and topics, the layout doesn't look crowded. One unusual thing you don't often see in speakers' web sites is the actual program evaluations from previous presentations. Another feature, which many web sites have, frequently asked questions (FAQs), is accessible in Susan Baker's web site. Her FAQs are also better than most.

Web Essential 10

Have an easy to find navigation bar. Use a bold, oversized capital letter to start paragraphs—like a drop cap. Making the first letter, word or phrase larger can create more attention and attract more readers. This can be easily done through Word. However, there is a word of caution. The use of a drop cap can sometimes cause spacing problems in some browsers. Just make sure you test before you apply.

Losing Element Site

A small custom product business web site has only one navigation tab on the bottom of the page. That's it. It's very small. However, in its defense the actual home page scrolls and the navigation bar stays static. One clever use of the font is to increase and boldface the size of the first letter to each paragraph's lead-in sentence.

Web Essentials 11

Use the home page as a kiosk, with links to dedicated feature copy pages rather than having the copy begin on the home page itself. Show graphics, such as a picture of an award, on the home page. Limit scrolling, which takes out the busy work of viewing the site. Place the navigation tabs at "eye level."

Winning Element Site

We discovered a site called Erie Insurance—*http://erieinsurance. com/*—with a home page we have never seen before. It is made of three sections of links—there is no body copy. The links are: *What's New at Erie Insurance, Insurance for You and Your Family*, and *Insurance for Your Business*. In addition, Erie Insurance has placed an animated graphic of its J. D. Power and Associates insurance award on the left side of the home page. The next useful element is the navigation bar. Rather than be on top or at the side, it's right smack dab in the middle of the page—as if you are looking at a file cabinet without having to bend down or crane your neck to look up. As you click on each tab, you see the subsections. This might be expensive to create, but we thought it was worth mentioning. Also, each tab is color coded like an organized office environment. A Related Topics menu on each page further adds to the well-organized appearance and functionality.

Web Essential 12

Make sure your links work. Don't make customers work so hard to find what they want.

Losing Element Site

We visited a small business trade site. Even the headline of its site says there are tools for the small shop. We were impressed because the site answered all the things you'd want from an industry portal—that is, a referral site—such as articles, products, industry links, news, and a bookstore. When you look for a product, the first thing the site gives you is a choice to search by keywords, product category, subcategory—or company. We don't want that many choices—you can confuse the customer. To make matters worse, you have to type in the keyword and then go through the hits. Too many decisions! When you finally make your choice, the site freezes. We tried it several times with the same results. At this point you lose interest and go back to Google.

Web Essential 13

A premade web site that includes content is what we refer to as a template on steroids. It's a great service provided that your level of exclusivity is protected. These sites are industry specific. They supply photos, FAQs, Ask the Pro, helpful hints, policies, ordering forms, anything that is universally used within your industry.

Winning Element Site (but with a Losing Element)

We discovered an industry within an industry: The supplying of prewritten content web sites that can be universally used by many businesses within the same industry. These turnkey canned content sites offer very limited customization. For example, a dentist can subscribe to a web site service that features *Ask the Dentist*, which answers dental questions that you enter via e-mail replies. This web site service package gives dentists who feature it on their site instant credibility and a plateau above their competition. It is an excellent and well done site. As we were about to write a kudo for this, we found out that *Ask the Dentist* can be found on many different dental practice pages. You can ask the same question and get the same answer—and it might not be the way the actual dental practice might do things. The answers are canned, stock replies. This isn't a bad thing. The only issue is one of exclusivity. We went to the supplier's site. It said each dental practice site received limited exclusivity per 20,000 people in its region. This means that in greater Boston alone there is a potential for well over a 100 of the same *Ask the Dentist* service sites.

If you are not in a metropolitan area, these types of sites are terrific. If you are in a metropolitan area, ask about exclusivity rights. We doubt very much that any service would want to have 100 sites in the same area. Just make sure.

Web Essential 14

Create a pinpointed mailing list. Provide education to your customers about the manufacturer.

Winning Element Site

What *Amazon.com* did for books *Zappos.com—www.zappos.com—* has done for shoes. Just as *Amazon.com* claims to have every book in print, Zappos' goal is to have every shoe available. This six-year-old company with 3 million customers now has warehouse space of more than one million feet—and it has the most utilitarian web site you've ever seen. Zappos boasts of carrying 90,000 different styles. And its list of manufacturers would fill a trade show book at a shoe show. The *wow* of the site is its vast inventory. Zappos is going after customers who know the brand and shoe styles that they like. It knows their fit and it caters to that need. When you click on a specific brand link, a page appears with the Zappos banner on top and what styles it sells for the desired brand. The site is a brand-focused site. The other neat feature is the ability to learn about each brand and to sign up for new information and styles that brand offers.

Web Essential 15

Offer the ability for customers to search your inventory to get exactly what they want, at a price they want to pay, and with their choice of delivery.

Winning Element Site

It would be difficult to list web site loser and winning elements and not mention *Blue Nile—www.BlueNile.com.* If someone told us 10 years ago that we could buy $25,000 diamonds online from a company only eight years old and doing over $100 million in business, we would have said that's crazy! But *Blue Nile* breaks all the rules. It did it with pure simplicity.

Someone once said, "When retailers rely only on flash and gimmicks to sell goods, they're in trouble because it takes away from the product they are selling." This site is clear, straightforward, and amazing. Other than this simplicity, there are few *wows* here with the exception of search capabilities. You can search for any one of 10 different shapes and *Blue Nile* will tell you the exact number of pieces it has in inventory and the price range. This site takes searching to another level. If you are look-ing for a round-shaped diamond, *BlueNile.com* found us 27,200 in stock with a price range of $339 to $701,828. But, of course, you can narrow your search within price ranges. When we did this search, between $5,000 to $9,000, we had a choice of 4,554. Each individual stone is listed by quality of cut, clarity, carat, polish, symmetry, report, and price.

Web Essential 16

Review your *About Us* page and look at the possibilities through the eyes of the Build-A-Bear mindset.

Winning Element Site

We also don't think it's possible to review exemplary web sites without looking at the Build-A-Bear Workshop site—*www. BuildABear. com*. With its popup menus and other features, it is one of the most sophisticated pieces of web design around. Its *About Us* page is a lesson for any *About Us* page on the web. It's maybe bigger than most people's web sites. *BuildABear.com* has subsections within the *About Us* page that are about the company, the mascot, about manufacturing processes, company foundation, awards, and community involvement. But the big-gest *wow* is still the interactive calendar of events. This is a web site unto itself. It's hard to find fault with anything on this site. So instead of finding fault, we'll just say it's a shame the won-derful community service work and the multitude of awards this company has earned are tucked away in pages that most people won't visit.

Web Essential 17

Offer a contest that links your business with a holiday or national "something" week. People will talk about it and your business.

Winning Element Site

MyPlumber.com—www.myplumber.com—features the *wow* of expertise and professionalism. *MyPlumber.com* hosts a grade school contest in conjunction with National Drinking Water Week. In addition, the *MyPlumber.com* water pipe logo, use of red-white-blue colors, ability to apply for work online, and so on, have this aura of authority and professionalism. Professionalism is hard to define, but we know it when we see it. That is, the company reveals online that it is large, with three different geographic territories, and has the expertise to take on any project, large or small.

When you review this site, you might be surprised we selected it as a Winning Element site, as it also uses Flash. We almost passed on it because of that. However, the Flash page is fast and not obnoxious in delivery. Besides, its other strengths outweighed this obvious distraction.

Web Essential 18

Add a personalized touch with an accent on education.

Winning Element Site

Although this is a $100 million plus web-based entertainment electronics business, Crutchfield—*www.crutchfield.com*—teaches some wonderful lessons. Number one, in the middle of its home page, Crutchfield has pictures of its employees and products, which certainly can't hurt morale and sales. Crutchfield has a category of *More Ways to Shop* that includes specials, gift cards, brand merchandise, and scratch-and-dent merchandise. Crutchfield also has a section on *Why Shop at Crutchfield.com* that is nice. It spells out what makes Crutchfield different and why it should be a customer's preferred choice. Very few businesses do this. The site also has the format we like—with a picture of the owner with a little welcome and a handwritten note. But the thing that really stands out about *Crutchfield.com* is the way it has embraced customer education and provides experts on call 24/7. These experts have a separate web site—*CrutchfieldAdvisor.com*—that offers 650 articles and videos of the products this retailer offers. That makes Crutchfield a winner in our book.

Web Essential 19
Have products that you can offer in different formats online.

Winning Element Site
Want to spend an enjoyable afternoon online? Go to *Art.com*—*www.art.com*. If you love art—and collecting art posters—you will love this site. The site navigation is mind blowing. By that we mean the sheer choices *Art.com* has for its shoppers. In fact, this company has created a *site of choices*. Not only does it show its stock—with 300,000 different images—but each one of those images can be ordered in over 50 different combinations, from image size to the kind of paper stock to real canvas to mounting, matting, and framing. It lets you visually create what you want online—it's really like play. If van Gogh saw all the things he could do with his work, he'd cut off his other ear! You can literally go from an inexpensive poster to a museum-quality copy.

Web Essentials 20
Use rotating testimonial quotes and small-space advertising blocks. Don't be afraid to expose yourself with your own writings or family pictures.

Winning Element Site
We wanted to review a consulting firm's site. The king of consultants and one of the brightest human beings on the planet is

Alan Weiss, Ph.D., and his firm, Summit Consulting—*www.summitconsulting.com.* Having read his books and listened to him speak, we feel he easily can be referred to as the father of modern-day consulting. Summit Consulting's home page is just a series of clickable boxes about upcoming workshops, seminars, and special features. Each box is a small advertising space, with advertising no more that an inch high and no more than an inch and half long, that is poignantly written and graphically different and inviting. Weiss's expertise is brilliantly illustrated with rotating quotations on the home page. *SummitConsulting.com* features an *About Alan Weiss* tab and then four pull-down menus about his services, his online store, his free articles, and his workshops. The site is not intimidating, which is a refreshing surprise because many of the professionals of Dr. Weiss's status would opt for an aloof, intellectual, and not very user friendly site. Another interesting tidbit is that on the same page that Weiss offers a *Million Dollar Consulting College* course with a five-figure price tag, he also has a place for pictures of his daughter's wedding.

SOME ADVICE FOR BUILDING A WINNING SITE

Take a few days or a few hours to look at different web sites. From the large business to small, from the consultant to the cabinetmaker, observe the similarities. Basic human motivations are relatively constant. But look for the thing that stands out, that is different, because after you say, "Wow!"—think, "That's what makes the critical difference."

Spend some time clicking on the navigation bar. Why? What makes or breaks a site may not pop up right away. You can overlook what sells and what doesn't. Sometimes we knew we liked a site, but we weren't quite sure why. We didn't notice, for example, Alan Weiss's revolving quotes until we almost clicked off the site. There are both obvious, in-your-face *wow* elements as well as subtle *wows* that create the pleasant surfing and shopping experience. The rich brown colors used on a cabinetmaker's site put us in the right mood. It was the white background in the diamond seller site that helped make the diamonds sparkle. It was whatever made us ask, "Why hadn't that been done before?" That was our feeling when we reviewed *Art.com* and *Zappos.com*. The *wow* is in online solutions that don't shout out. They are understated and focused on visitors. They make the site user friendly and a place in which you feel comfortable visiting—and you don't even know why. What we are challenging you to do is dig down a little deeper to find out why.

Chapter 8's Essential Essentials

1. Make your site convenient and user friendly.
2. Break your offering down into logical chunks of information.
3. Take your customer age into account when planning the readability of your site.
4. Don't focus on the price as the first thing.
5. Personalize your site in every way you can.
6. An unprofessional web site hurts you rather than helps you even if you have a high Google ranking.
7. Accept charge cards.
8. If you received an award, place a picture of it on your home page.
9. Let technology work for your customers to make buying online easy.

Chapter 8's Essential Essentials, *continued*

10. Have an easy to find navigation bar.
11. Offer a contest that associates your business with a holiday or "national something" week.
12. Review your *About Us* page and look at the possibilities.
13. Offer the ability for customers to search your inventory to get exactly what they want, at a price they want to pay, and their choice of delivery.
14. Create a pinpointed mailing list.

For more information on this topic, go to

www.essentialonlinesolution.com.

Step III

Positioning You as the Source: Creating Expert Status

Chapter 9

E-mail Marketing or Is It Pinpoint Marketing?

Sometimes when you start writing a chapter or article on a topic you are passionate about, you just want to explode with the facts and your feelings. You want to shake the reader and say: This is the important stuff. This is the stuff that will turn your business. It will bring it to the next level. You write an outline and you see yourself writing "the most important aspect of..." and then you realize another part is just as important. This is the case in this chapter. It has so many important parts and to place one in front of another, sounds like we are saying one is more important. This is not the case.

This is a chapter that combines many traditional marketing values and concepts with a dose of common sense mixed together with some high-tech spice to create killer ways to promote a business. However, the goals are *contemporary traditional*. We think that's a new term, so let us explain what that means. To do that, we need to share a bit of advertising history.

Advertising was once limited to newspapers and magazines to deliver the sales pitch to many people at once. Then came radio and TV. With the advent of personal computers, word processing, and database marketing, direct mail advertising became more practical, especially for smaller businesses. It made it possible to virtually advertise to the world. Individual customers could be pinpointed rather than large market segments. With the use of the mail merge feature in Microsoft Word, for example, it became easy and inexpensive to send out personalized messages.

But bulk mail advertising came with an ever-higher price and delivery problems at the post office. There is also no end to how much you can spend on creating beautiful color direct mail pieces.

Then came e-mail and it was utopia. There was little cost for the actual piece and the delivery costs were free. It's boom time. The flood gates opened to anyone who had something to sell and cyberspace was flooded with e-mails.

Popups!

Then, of course, the dreaded popup message started to appear on everyone's computer. We don't recommend or even discuss popup advertising because it is frequently suppressed by today's filters and still is considered an annoyance. So don't even think of going there!

E-ZINES

So what's the best way to use the powerful Internet mediums? There are different approaches that work exceptionally well. Common to all of them are:

- Sharing knowledge
- Creating benefit rather than a hard sell

If you constantly send out price pieces, sale ads, and promotions, the reader will start to ignore them and eventually block or unsubscribe to your e-mailings.

Remember, a big part of using the web is still research. People are looking for knowledge, things to learn. Web users—your prospects—are statistically better educated and more affluent than the general public. Gimmicks and tricks only go so far. That is why you should become a source of knowledge—position yourself as the expert. The best way to do this is the e-mail version of the Internet newsletter—better known as the *e-zine*. It only makes sense—newsletters have always worked. E-zines do, too, and they are much easier to publish and cost far less because you don't have to print them.

Here is a winning format for e-zines:

1. *A short article of interest to your reader—something interesting and provocative.* This is what will make you an industry expert, and industry experts command respect as well as higher fees and prices. We pay extra to work with experts. Make the article between 500 and 750 words. It will be difficult at first, but it becomes fun. Asking questions and then answering them in your newsletter is a great format to showcase your abilities.
2. *A quote.* There are lots of interesting quotes online and it just adds a nice touch that people love to read.
3. *A news item—something about your industry or community.* Don't confuse this with your main article. It's just a short report of what is happening.

4. *A price offering—some type of incentive or sale.* By the time the reader gets to this point, you already have credibility and your readers will perceive your offering as good service or will just respect you for being price sensitive.

Number 5 is the secret weapon. It is what makes the e-zine "sticky," a place where prospects want to return. People just don't think about it.

5. *A joke or cartoon.* This will build an e-zine faster than any other way, yet people sometimes scoff at the use of humor. *Playboy* features jokes. The *New Yorker* has cartoons. The editorial pages of newspapers have political cartoonists. Comic relief creates a connection. Do you need to hire a gagman or a cartoonist? No. *Cartoonbank.com* and other sites will supply you with more jokes and cartoons than you can ever use.

These five components make your e-zine marketing read, position you as an expert, and help to build your brand.

How often do you send out your e-mail e-zine? It depends on your type of business. Consultants and professionals might want to send one weekly or every other week. Once a month or quarterly works, too, for some businesses. But anything beyond that and it's not a newsletter. Whatever you decide, be consistent with the timing of your delivery. Always send your e-zine on the same day of the week or date of the month.

E-MAIL MARKETING ESSENTIALS

We have just shared with you what we consider to be the most powerful tool available on- and offline, the e-newsletter. It works for almost every business we can think of, from plumbers giving tips to accountant discussing changes in the tax code.

Other essentials of e-mail marketing exist:

1. *Name collection.* What's your strategy for gathering names and building your e-mail list? How do you ask for names? When do you ask? Why should someone give you this information and what's in it for him or her? The greater the reward, the greater the willingness to sign up. These are the questions that need to be answered. Unfortunately, the verdict is out on buying e-mail lists. Yes, plenty of companies sell them; but the success rates are not yet conclusive. But, only time will tell whether they give the same value as traditional mailing lists.

   A good way to build your list is through promotions or offers that require some type of sign in. Don't try to trick someone into giving you his or her e-mail information—it only bites you back later. The best way is through strategic alliances with other businesses that are marketing to the same customer. Sometimes a mere mention in a newsletter or a link is all that it will take to entice someone to partnering with you. Foster these relationships and befriend the best marketers.

   Don't forget past customers. We know it sounds obvious, but unfortunately these customers don't always make it to the list. Just make sure they are not slipping through your fingers.

2. *Alignment—styles, graphics, and fonts.* Like a mantra, our research on e-mail marketing revealed that the marketing piece reinforces the image and brand of the company. This is called *alignment.* Make sure your e-mails have the same look and feel as the rest of your company marketing

materials. The reason we like the term *alignment* goes back to taking those simple tests in school that went like this: "Look at these five times and tell me which ones don't fit." People can tell what's wrong faster than knowing what's right. Be consistent with your styles, graphics, and fonts, and you'll always look professional.

3. *Opt in and out procedures—unsubscribe and subscribe.* If there is one aspect on e-mail marketing and building a list that can cause you more aggravation and time, it is not having a clearly defined procedure for signing people up to your mailing list. You must be able to confirm that they want to be on the list. You must have a clear procedure for anyone to unsubscribe. The key is to automate this process as much as possible. Entering e-mail addresses yourself leads to wrong or false addresses. To automate this, try such applications as Constant Contact *(www.constantcontact.com)* with the cooperation of your webmaster. Also, be sure to follow the rules and regulations for e-mail privacy. Visit the Direct Marketing Association's site for a free privacy policy generator *(//www.the-dma.org/privacy/creating.shtml)*. Be aware of the Can Spam Law, officially known as Controlling the Assault of Non-Solicited Pornography and Marketing Act.

Can Spam

Visit the federal government's web site for details at http://www.ftc.gov/bcp/conline/pubs/buspubs/canspam.htm.

---

4. *The subject line.* The subject line is one of those topics that many people feel should be the first thing discussed.

Perhaps it is because if there is any one element that will determine your success or failure, it will be a well-written subject line. We define well-written as short, interesting, concise, and what promises a benefit or solution to the reader. The greatest headline ever written was "Get Rich Quick." Let that be your model for great subject lines. What does your reader want as fast as they can get it?

The best way to get good subject lines is to look at the ones you get in your Inbox. Which ones do you open and which ones make you want to hit delete key? There are certain keywords that are automatically picked up by spam filters. The biggest one, interestingly enough, is *free*. (How ironic, since so much of the web is or seems to be *for free*.)

5. *Copy, copy, copy.* Here it is again. It's all about the copy, all about the words. Graphics are great, copy sells. Remember Mark Twain's famous line? "If I had more time, I would have made it shorter." Great copy is concise and effective and makes you want to keep on reading.

Short and Sweet

A great primer about great copywriting is 87 Marketing Secrets of the Written Word *by Ted Nicholas, which can be obtained at* www.tednicholas.com. *You can also sign up there for his free newsletter and see more word magic.*

---

6. *Headlines.* By headlines we mean subject headings and any place in your site where you can enlarge or bold text to grab attention. We'd rather have too many headlines than not enough. People read headlines. They read the **bold**. It breaks text up and makes it **more readable**. It

makes your copy **user friendly**. Great communication is not like the Indianapolis 500, a race that constantly goes around in a circle, but rather 24 hours at Le Mans that slows down and accelerates. That's what a headline will do. **It's putting down the accelerator and shouting what you are saying.** It demands attention. It is the **secret weapon of great copywriters**.

7. *Modified long copy and the sales letter*. Modified long copy in a sales letter is simply writing copy using short paragraphs (four to six lines) with a keyword or phrase CAPITALIZED, underlined, or in **bold**. The letter must have a postscript or a series of P.S.'s that are also CAPITALIZED, underlined, or in **bold**. When a sales letter is read on paper, people have the tendency to read from the bottom to the top. With e-mail such copy enhancements are like using headlines. Here you can highlight text within a paragraph, The benefit is that when a person reads a letter with headlines and modified long copy, they see what the writer wants them to see: the important parts to read. People may ask, "Why don't you just put down the key phrases and shorten the whole thing?" It makes sense, but it just doesn't work.

8. *Know the numbers*. What's your conversion rate? There are a number of statistics you can gather about your e-mail marketing pieces. Some basics statistics are:

- Pieces actually delivered
- How many opened
- How many forwarded

When Rick sends out his weekly e-zine he has one person who forwards his e-mail 147 times. He also has eight other people who forward his e-zine 50-plus times.

This is information that can be extremely valuable in your marketing. An interesting statistic is the number of people who open your e-mail and then click to your web site. You can also find out how many took the desired action you wanted such as sign up for a free trial, sign up for a free tour, sign up for a free class, or buy the product or service. Once you know how many prospects become purchasers, you can create your *conversion rate number*. For example, 1,000 prospects get your e-mail. Of them, 100 prospects open the e-mail. At this point, you have 10 percent readership. Then ten of these prospects click the link to visit your web page. Finally, of these prospects, two individuals actually make a purchase. That means you have a 20 percent conversion rate of those ten prospects who visited your web site. The downside, of course, in this scenario, is that only 10 percent of the people opened the original e-mail. Can you imagine how it could affect your sales if 20 percent did? It all goes back to good copy.

9. *Linking to what—Where will they land?* Where prospects land means what part of your web site they click to open. Most online business e-mailings link the home page—don't do that. It's a common mistake. Direct prospects to where they will take action. If you are sending out an e-mail marketing message that sells that super-duper new drain plunger we told you about, sending prospects to the home page only delays the sales process. Link them to the page that offers additional sales information about the product or service and the way the site visitor can purchase. In other words, make it easy and convenient to buy. That is what online sales is all about.

10. *Add a survey or poll.* Engage potential customers by providing a link to a survey or poll. Your e-mail then serves

to solicit their opinion. Surveys work the best when you show the results of the survey instantly. In many cases this is enough to get potential customers to participate. You can ask, for example, those *USA Today*-kind of questions such as "Are business conditions the same as last year? Falling behind last year? A little better than last year? Significantly beating last year?" It's a nice piece of marketing, too, because you create a relationship with the customer—and the cost is minimal. You can use a *SurveyMonkey.com—www.survyemonkey.com*—and similar online survey vendors to poll 100 people or less at a time for free or purchase a survey package.

11. *The art of strategic alliances, mentions, and referrals.* The best source to collect new e-mail addresses comes from strategic alliances you have with other businesses selling non-competing products with the same customer base. We mentioned earlier that a mere mention of your web site and contact information can affect your lists favorably. When another list recommends or sends out a story specifically about your product, your sales can go through the roof, especially if the company doing the referring has a well-populated list that gives you lots of exposure. Form your alliances carefully and make them win-win for both parties. If you don't want to refer a particular company, then don't accept an offer from it. When Rick sends out his e-zine and he mentions a Microsoft product, the recipients' clicks almost instantly register at the software giant's web site.

12. *Until they buy or die.* There is a constant theme among aggressive marketing people: Keep sending prospects information until they die or buy. In short, never throw away a prospect. Just try a different approach. Obviously

there is debate about this. If someone on your mailing list has not purchased anything, maybe you should take the hint and strike them off?

The rub here is that cheap can be expensive. It's a major problem with e-mail marketing. Even if you use a service, the price is cheap—and the government is still not taxing e-mail yet. Then there are those less-than-finely tuned e-mail lists of qualified prospects. You may think you are sending out 5,000 e-mails, but 1,000 of those names are people who could care less about you or your business. You may not care. Hey, it's so cheap and you don't care how many you send out. However, e-mail soliciting gets expensive when you run the risk of turning off customers by sending them a sales pitch they have no interest in reading. Then there are the kind customers should not see.

When Rick bought his home in Florida, he needed to furnish a complete house. When he went into a furniture store, he fell in love with the merchandise and the people. Of course, Rick, being the marketer that he is, automatically signed up to receive marketing messages and e-zines. The next week he received an e-zine announcing a sale for 20% off. Imagine how he felt! And imagine how the store owner felt when he had to refund the difference to the sale price! If it wasn't for cheap e-mails and sloppy mailing lists, the message might not have gone out to Rick. Cheap was very expensive for the furniture store that day.

Spammer or Good Guy?

You do not want to be viewed by your potential customers as a spammer. This is not the label you want to carry with you.

Chapter 9's Essential Essentials

1. Share knowledge and create a benefit to the reader in every e-mail marketing campaign.
2. Use the same standard format every time.
3. Designate a consistent day of the week or month that you send out your e-mail campaign.
4. Implement a name collection strategy.
5. Align your e-mail marketing with your company look and feel.
6. Be current with all laws concerning opt-in and -out procedures.
7. Copy is king.
8. Use modified long copy when writing your e-mail marketing message.
9. Learn and use the data from your conversion rate to build sales.
10. Link to the page on your site where you want the sales action to happen.

For more information on this topic, go to

www.essentialonlinesolution.com.

Chapter 10

The Blog

The Tool that Can Change Your Business

What is a blog? Why would I want one?

Blogs sound like a science fiction movie monster, don't they? And why would a down-to-earth independent small business owner want something that sounds like a *blob*?

So what is a blog? Take instant messaging, add a web page, and you have a blog. Blog is just short for weblog. Think of a blog as a diary or a journal on a particular topic, your thoughts and observations, tips and ideas, whatever is on your mind that can be easily updated by you the author. According to Andy Wibbels, author of *Easy Bake Weblogs*—*www.easybakeweblogs.com*—"A blog is an easy, instantly and frequently updated web site, focused around a topic, industry, or personality."

How did weblogs or blogs get started? In the late 1990s, three guys in California—and not in a garage this time—created software that did not require any skill with HTML code, the language that web designers use to "write" a site. (For people like Rick and Barbara, that comes as a big relief.) Basically, it allows people to type and press enter to add text messages to a running list of entries—an electronic diary. Seeing the potential for fostering community, the source code was offered for free. People loved it because the software not only made web sites readable without having to have a programmer, sites required no hosting fees, just an Internet connection.

Blogs gathered momentum during the highly charged political atmosphere of the early 2000s. Bloggers (people who blog) started to express their opinions online about political candidates and issues. Soon, for many people, blogs became a primary source of information and even took market share away from the mainstream media. In 2004, Merriam-Webster dictionary made *blog* the word of the year. In case you're wondering, blogosphere is that borderless nation of blogs where Bloggers go to blog or to post comments on other people's blogs.

In May 2005, *BusinessWeek* ran a cover story, "Blogs Will Change Your Business," which caught the business world by surprise. It reported that some 9 million blogs exist with 40,000 new ones each day! As of September 2005, a blog search engine tracked 16.5 million blogs. As of January 2006, 24.9 million blogs were out there. Yes, you read that right. (There are search engines that only search for blogs.) That shows you how blogs have grown in importance. Blogs exist for virtually every kind of subject you can imagine. Sometimes more than one blog grows up around its subject. Harry Potter certainly has more than one!

Are blogs good for business, you might ask? Take a look at General Motors Vice Chairman Bob Lutz's Fast Lane blog—*http://fastlane.gmblogs.com*—where General Motors lets you in on the latest designs, models, and entries into the Le Mans car race. Bob also taps into other GM resources to tell the GM story and future direction of the company. New Hampshire's Stonyfield Farm is the largest organic yogurt company in the world. It has a full time chief blogger who writes five blogs for the company as a means of building brand loyalty—*http://stonyfield.com/weblog.* Sun Microsystems, which produces operating system software, servers, and computers, uses its blogs internally for project teams to work together sharing information or to keep the company updated on projects. Sun Microsystems has over 2,000 employee blogs.

Why would a small business person bother with a blog? Here are some good reasons:

- Free or low cost
- Easy to use
- Fast updates
- Drives traffic to your web site
- Two-way interaction with customers
- Positions you as an expert
- Branding
- Receive higher ranks on search engines
- Build reputation
- For showing a personal side
- For making a primary web site

Make it your web site? Why not? No programming is required—and no web developer, no graphic designer—and just an Internet connection is needed to have a blog. Wow, who could ask for more?

Blogs are low-fee (and sometimes no-fee) and easy to use. You can create a blogging web site in less time than you can drive to the store for a carton of milk. Rick has created blogs for retailers in less than 10 minutes using Blogger *(www.Blogger.com)* and it's free.

Blogs are used by businesses as a part of their online marketing strategy to:

- Have a personal conversation with customers
- Engage customers
- Get feedback from customers and prospects
- Introduce new products in the industry or their own product (in a subtle way)
- Comment on what's happening in the industry
- Give opinions about items, books, news in the media that impact your customer
- Place e-newsletters on blogs—Rick does this at *http:// ricksegelsblog.blogspot.com*

With a blog, you increase your web presence and give customers another reason to e-mail friends your information. Search engines love good, regularly updated web content so the blog's chances of being recognized by Google and the others are increased.

Someone asked us, "Is there a difference between a blog for personal use and one for business?" We answered a big *yes*! Here's where your marketing strategy comes into play. If you want to be recognized as an expert accountant, speaker, financial planner, electrician, or polarity practitioner, it would be in your best interest to have a business blog. To be effective, a blog needs your conver-

---

What Do We Say on Our Blogs?

Rick does a nice job of blending his everyday adventures with marketing and customer service and giving his opinions and tips. Barbara takes her cues from her business contacts, books, and articles and then gives her opinions and asks questions.

sational style. That way your personality will come out. However, telling us what you did on the weekend with your kids does not relate to your business. It distracts from your branding initiative.

Right now there is no better online option than a blog to get your message out for *free*. If you know of another one, let us know.

The major difference between a web site and a blog is that each blog entry—called a *post*—has its own unique Internet address and it is easily and immediately uploaded to the blog. Because each post is a unique entry, when someone types a keyword into a search engine that matches up with something you wrote in your post, it shows up in the search results.

Copy is king. Where have you heard that before? It's still true for compelling blogs that people want to visit again and again. Check out Terry Brock's Your Success blog for some marketing insights and copy—*www.yoursuccess.blogspot.com.* Another blog example: Steve Shapiro's *Goal-Free Living* book blog *http://goalfreeliving.com*

Customers feel that your blog adds value as long as you supply good quality content. You are letting them "in" on secrets, tips, ideas, or opinions that help them. In fact, they'll tell others and send your blog's address along to them. Click and send. Remember the adage "Give to get"? Do that in your blog and you will not have any problems with customers feeling it's a fad or you're trying to sell them something.

BLOGS AND E-NEWSLETTERS

You might be thinking, "What about the e-newsletter I'm currently doing or I'm thinking of doing? How does a blog differ from an e-newsletter? Are blogs better or worse?"

Actually you can do both! Or you can just do one or the other. It's up to you and your marketing strategy. Rick decided to fill his blog with his e-newsletter, so he attracts bloggers who would not have received his e-newsletter. Barbara does not have an e-newsletter—but she has a blog.

Both online mediums are good to stay in contact with your customers and prospects. And, we think a blog is a good tool to add to your marketing strategy and get your message out to online public and customers alike.

You can jump right in, as the members of Rick's Mastermind group did when he challenged them to set up their own blogs. Barb, a Mastermind member, already had her blog up—even before Rick did. It is that easy.

GETTING READY TO START

A more methodical way to start is to explore the world of blogs first. Then create your blog.

Read Blogs

Start by reading blogs. Many web sites exist that just catalog and allow you to search the blogosphere for different blogs:

- *Technorati.com*
- *Blogexplosions.com*
- *Blogdex.com*
- *GlobeOfBlogs.com*
- *Feedster.com*
- *Icerocket.com*

Type in a topic or subject that's in your field of interest. You can also use traditional search engines such as Google and Yahoo! by adding the keyword *blog*.

If you are a financial planner, you might type in *financial planning* and discover several blogs devoted to this topic. See what people are saying. You might find a topic to talk about in your own blog just by reading what others are discussing.

Decide Your Blog's Style of Writing

You can also read blogs to get a sense of what writing style is most suited for your blog. Here are some examples:

- *Conversational.* Visit *http://leadershiplady.blogspot.com,* Barb's blog on leadership.
- *Informational.* See *www.bizzbangbuzz.com.*
- *Selling.* See *www.goalfreeliving.com.*
- *Combination.* See *http://ricksegelsblog.blogspot.com.*

Placement of Data on Blog

What kind of look and feel do you want for your blog? What do you think your customers or prospective customers would find appealing?

- Left- or right-side layout
- Bio, picture, links, etc.

Colors for Your Blog

Some blogs are so dark it's hard to read them. Other blogs are clear and crisp and almost say hello. What colors say hello to you and your business?

- Match web site or brand.
- Use a color scheme that would appeal to the top 20 percent of your customer base.

Comment on Some Blogs

Go ahead, it won't hurt. Try your hand at posting comments on blogs that you like. See how easy it is to post a blog entry.

HOW DO YOU SET UP A BLOG

What is the process for setting up and writing a blog? Figure 10.1 shows you how—and here are the steps used for web-hosting services that provide automated blog creation software. These steps are similar to many services such as Blogger, a division of Google.

1. Sign up for your blog.
2. Provide your profile information.
3. Select a template for your blog site.
4. Write your blog entry.
5. Review for typos.
6. Press Publish.

Choose Your Blog Service
Visit free and fee-based blog-creating sites to see what they offer. Just starting out? Go for the free site to get your feet wet. Why spend money when testing the waters? Some major players are shown in Table 10.1.

Create Your Blog!
If you've done your homework you'll just check these items off, if not take a few minutes to review the key decisions you'll need to make *before* you start the process.

Figure 10.1 Creating a Blog

Table 10.1 Major Blog Creation Sites

Free blog creation sites

Blogger.com (The first free blogging site, which is now owned by Google.)

Blogexplosion.com

Spaces.msn.com

Fee-based blog creation sites

Typepad.com

SquareSpace.com

Name of Blog

Choose carefully. Does it say what you want people to know? You can use your own name if you do business that way—for example, Kim Snider's blog at *http://blog.kimsnider.com*. You can have a product name. Steve Shapiro did this by using the title of his book *Goal-Free Living* at *http://goalfreeliving.com*. Or you can use a topic name such as *Brownie Points* at *www.browniepointsblog.com*.

Colors of Blog

Are you going with your company colors? You may need a fee-based service and a web designer for that option. Free service sites usually have only a selection of predesigned choices. Either way, select the color scheme that best fits your brand color scheme. Don't use more than three colors. You'll just confuse the eye.

Format

What look do you want: contemporary, newsy, formal, laid-back? If you are a financial planner, choosing a casual look might not work with building the trust your prospects expect. Review formats so that you can choose what says *hello* to you—and best fits your style, message, and brand. Consider using three columns or two columns. What about data on the left column versus data on right column? Should you include related links? Your customer base—and the content you want to deliver—determines the format. A New Hampshire sign company uses two columns to set off its running blog and what essentially is its business web site—see *http://signsneversleep.typepad.com*.

Description

Provide visitors with a brief introduction that tells them the purpose of your blog. Be conversational rather than too formal. For examples, check out *http://candle-maker.blogspot.com* ("Candle making supplies blog for my web site. New ideas, new creations, just blogging about candles.") and *www.hiring-revolution.com* ("Hiring Revolution tackles issues that affect human resources professionals, hiring managers and industry employment in general.").

Profile

Enter your company's information—such as your name, bio, and interesting tidbits.

Picture

Provide a picture of your business, your product, even one of you if you are the product or service. Generate interest and a reason to buy.

Post Your First Entry

Announcing the blog and why you decided to enter into this online medium might be a good place to start.

You can post this yourself. From the moment you create your blog to anywhere you happen to be and at any time: in the middle of the night, at the airport, even from a phone! The beauty of the blog is the ability to post without having to go through a techie to get it done. You can also write a week's worth of material and have the automated blog service post different entries at the time and day you designate.

It may make sense to pay your web developer to do this if you are too busy and it makes good business sense to outsource that work.

Now, send an announcement to everyone you know to check out your new blog. Barbara and Rick also place their blog links in the signature line of their e-mails. Always give people the opportunity to visit you. Just make it part of your signature.

Feed Your Blog

How much time does it really take to maintain your blog?

As little and as much time as you'd like. Rick faithfully writes his blog once a week. He began by having blogs written ahead of time. Now he likes the challenge of using what's happened to him that week to write in his blog. Barbara posts on her blog each Monday morning. She is not as faithful as Rick. Whatever you decide, stick to the regimen. Once a week is good. Every day is great. Posting once a month is okay. What works for your business and industry will work in the blogosphere. Just be consistent.

Barbara interviewed Sheryl Lindsell-Roberts, president of a business writing consultancy:

> A blog is not a big commitment of time in view of the return. If you're not going to write or if you don't like writing them having a blog is tedious. Don't do it.

For more of her ideas, check out her article "Blogs for Beginners" at *www.Sherylwrites.com/pages/ARTCLblg.html.*

Remember conversational style is the best to use when posting to your blog. You want your prospects and customers to feel like they are having a conversation with you. They get to know your personality and feel like they already know you when it comes time for them to do business and buy from you. A blog helps you to build trust.

Dan Crowther, in his article that says it all, "How To Instantly Get Your Business Blog Postings to Show Up in the Search Engines and Generate Tons of Free Search Engine Traffic to Your Site," recommends adding keywords that you expect your prospects and customers to enter when they conduct searches for products and services. They need to be part of the blog title, first sentence, and a couple of more times through the blog. Don't overdo it. Crowther also recommends that you write postings that are 250 words or more, which is longer than normal blog postings. That's because he says search engines don't really like short entries as this is the tactic of spammers.

BLOGGING 201

So what happens after you create your blog? How do you get hits on your blog? How do you get your blog noticed? How do you make the blog work for your business?

There are several ways to increase your visibility. You can get an RSS feed. You can list your blog on search engines. You can make comments on other blogs and add your blog's address. We have already mentioned keywords and adding a blog site link to your web site and e-mail. There are also TrackBacks and carnivals. Let's begin with RSS feeds.

RSS Feeds

RSS what? When we first heard of RSS feeds, we thought it was something that would be way over our readers' heads. Actually it's not. Just take an RSS feed step by step and you'll be fine.

According to *www.webreference.com*, Really Simple Syndication (RSS) is a lightweight XML format designed for sharing headlines and other web content. Think of it as a distributable "What's New" for your site.

By using an RSS feed, you can have your posts picked up by interested customers and prospects without having to go through spamming software and the like—your customers get it on demand and choose to have your updates sent to them automatically. The papergirl delivers it right to your computer.

There are books written just on RSS feeds. We just want to say make sure you add one to your blog.

How?

Each blog service has a different process. Usually it is as simple as clicking the Site Feed tab, button, or option, and selecting *Publish Site Feed.*

RSS Readers

Okay, I have the RSS feed idea now. How can I *read* an RSS feed? You need a free RSS reader—you knew that was coming—and download it to your computer. RSS feed readers let you sign up for and retrieve blogs easily, comfortably, and efficiently in a dedicated program, on a web site, or in your e-mail program.

Search the Internet with the keywords *RSS feed readers* to find the latest and greatest. Here are some that are currently available and easy to use:

- *Newsgater.com*—free
- *FeedDemon.com*—$29.95

Listing Your Blog with Search Engines

Listing your blog is similar to listing your web site. By doing so, the world knows you and your blog exist, and when you post, they update your listing.

Enter your blog address in three blog search engines a day. This way, you'll be listed in the major ones—as well as the lesser-known ones and any new blog search engines that come online.

Here are the top blog search engines to list your blog in:

- *Technocarti.com*
- *Pubsub.com*
- *BlogLines.com*
- *Blogwise.com*
- *Google.com*
- *Yahoo.com*
- *BlogDigger.com*

Adding your blog is really easy. Copy your blog's URL and paste it into the appropriate box. Click ADD and you're all done.

Linking Your Blog to Your Web Site

Here's another way to draw traffic to your web site and get noticed by the search engines. Link your blog to your web site—preferably to the pages that sell products—pages on which prospects do what you want them to do: Buy.

Get the Most Out of Your Blog

Advertise your products on your blog. Show a picture and include 25 to 100 words that tactfully compel your blog reader to click to your web site in order to find out more.

More Blogging 201

Blogs are maturing and there will always be new things to learn about them. Here are sources to check out what's hot today:

- *Web Logs*—http://weblogs.about.com
- *Dan Crowther*—http://101publicrelations.com/ bloggingforbusiness.html
- *Andy Wibbels*—http://andywibbels.com

Place *Goggle Ad sense* on your blog. This is where you make money from other people's products. They can be related products to what you offer or just merchandise and services you like.

Crosslink your blog to other people's blogs. Find like-minded people who have blogs and see if you can arrange to link your blog to theirs and vice versa. Conduct an advance search on Yahoo! or Google to locate, for example, "financial planner"—but make sure in the advance settings that you filter for those results that have RSS/XML. You will then get results that will for the most part only include financial planners who have blogs. You'll be amazed at what you find.

Blogrolling is placing other blog links that you like on your blog. This is considered good etiquette. It is the same as making referrals. To see a blogroll, check out *www.hiring-revolution.com.*

TrackBack is a mechanism that enables you to let a blogger know if you wrote something about his or her blog. It's like sending a CC'ed e-mail. According to Sheila Ann Manuel Coggins of *Weblogs.about.com:*

> It is a remote commenting system between blogs. This is used when an individual reads an entry in someone's blog and chooses

to write about that entry in his or her own blog. When TrackBack is used, a ping will be sent to the originator of the post, so he or she will know who blogged about his or her blog entry.

Not all blogging software gives you the ability to use TrackBack.

Permalink gives you the ability to include a link to an information source that you have quoted or included in your blog. That way, blog readers can click to see the source, such as an online business journal article. The Permalink, as you can guess, stays on the post and is not lost when the next post in entered.

Then there is the newest way to blog for business, the *carnival blog*. Think of it as a real carnival, with all kinds of things to do and see and moving from one town to another. A blog carnival, however, moves from topic to topic. It involves many bloggers getting together and one blogger hosting the blog for one topic and then, over the next week or month, a new carnival blogger hosts and a new topic takes over. To see an example, visit Consumerism Commentary—*www.consumerismcommentary.com/carnival_of_personal_finance.*

Blogs to Watch and Learn From

- *AdRants.com—www.adrants.com*—covers marketing topics
- *StartWithALead.com—http://blog.startwithalead.com*—marketing
- *WindsorMedia.com—http://windsormedia.blogs.com/lipsticking*—online marketing to women
- *BizzBangBuzz.com—http://bizzbangbuzz.blogspot.com*—covers legal profession topics
- *www.icblind.com*—graphic design firm
- *Luxist.com—www.luxist.com*—surveys luxury travel

- Seth Godin—*http://sethgodin.typepad.com*—marketing and because he is just plain interesting
- *BostonUncorked.com*—*www.bostonuncorked.com*—wine tasting club

Let's recap. Blogs are not sci-fi monsters and they can change your business. We didn't give you any political blogs—but we could have. Your decisions and applications of the knowledge you now have about blogs and blogging will help you drive bottom-line results. Remember, the distinct advantage of a blog is to give your customers an "insider" look into yourself and your world. Your personality will shine through and get them excited to know what's going on in the business, the industry and yourself. Here's to a fantastic business blog. Yours!

Chapter 10's Essential Essentials

1. Be clear on the business reasons for having a blog.
2. Use your copywriting skills to attract people to read your blog.
3. Use a blog as a depository place for your e-zine or newsletter. Recycling at its best.
4. Read other businesspeople's blogs to get a feel for what you'd like your writing to sound like. Comment on the other people's blogs to drive traffic to your blog or web site.
5. Brand your blog just like you do all your other marketing materials. Be consistent as much as possible.

Chapter 10's Essential Essentials, *continued*

6. Start with a free blog to get the hang of it.
7. Decide how often to "feed" your blog. Daily? Weekly?
8. Use RSS feeds and readers.
9. List your blog with search engines.
10. Get the most out of your blog with blogrolling, blog car-nivals, TrackBack, and the like.

For more information on this topic, go to

www.essentialonlinesolution.com.

Chapter 11

Podcasting

The Sweet Sounds of Success

What is your customer's most precious possession? Before you start rattling off lists of cars, homes, jewelry, let us stop you. The most precious thing your customers have is their time. (And, perhaps, their iPod, which we will get to in a moment.)

That's why small business owners work so hard to capture even the smallest fragment of the customer's day. A few minutes of undivided attention, where you can speak directly to your clients, address their concerns, and offer solutions to their problems are priceless.

Now imagine you've got that time. You've got some one-on-one time with your consumers as they go about household chores or make the morning commute to the office. Best of all, you're not only reaching your target audience, but they're eager to hear everything you've got to say—and are even signing up for more.

Sounds too good to be true. Yet the technology to deliver this target audience is already in place. True, it's still in its infancy, only appearing on the web late in 2004. Nevertheless, creation and distribution systems are constantly improving as end users and designers refine the system.

Welcome to the World of Podcasting.

Oh, did we mention that it's nearly free?

WHAT IS PODCASTING?

Like many of the technologies discussed throughout the book, podcasting is both an art and a science. In a nutshell, podcasting involves creating audio files—similar to miniradio broadcasts—that can be accessed by anyone online. Listeners download these files to play back on an iPod or other kind of digital media player—they can even choose to listen to them live at your web site via streaming media. Most podcasts are just a few minutes long. Some have been known to stretch as long as 60 minutes or more. The RSS feeds discussed in the earlier chapter allow listeners to sign up for new files, providing you with ongoing access into their lives.

Podcasts can be used to discuss anything and everything. There are podcasts covering the broadest possible interests—sports, cars, politics and technologies—and catering to the narrowest of niche markets. There are podcasts covering the lives of individual zoo animals. You can broadcast in any language. There are podcasts in English, Japanese, and German, but there are also podcasts in Icelandic, Mohawk, and other even less common languages.

Unlike a live radio show, creating podcasting's audio files is easy to do. At a bare minimum, you need a computer, a microphone, an Internet connection, and something to say. We're going to split this chapter into two sections. One will address the content—that's the art. The other section discusses the technology, programs, distribution, and promotion of your podcast. That's the science.

HOW CAN I USE PODCASTING IN MY SMALL BUSINESS?

The key to podcasting is to view it as a communication tool to connect you with your customers. They're giving you their time and a portion of their attention—it's up to you to provide content that they'll find of value. Do this, and you've taken a critical first step in building a valuable business relationship.

It helps to be entertaining. After all, reading the dictionary is useful and instructive, especially if you're trying to build your vocabulary. Yet it's also dead-dog boring. No one's going to turn in to listen. But if you format the dictionary reading in an exciting, engaging way—perhaps as a quiz show, or by building a series of interviews around theme words—you'll get listeners.

How can you apply this to your small business? After all, chances are you're not selling dictionaries. But someone in real estate could offer audio tour guides of all the homes in his or her territory. Motivational speakers or coaches could deliver mini-seminars, whetting the consumer's appetite for longer, more in-depth sessions. Insurance agents, physicians, attorneys, and others who stand on business's frontline could use podcasts as story-telling opportunities, discussing real-life or theoretical case studies and offering solutions based on their own expertise.

An example of a product-based podcast is Centennial Wines. We went to Google and typed in the keywords *podcast* and *retail* and found on Podcast News this information on Centennial wine store:

> In the podcast, James Moll, Centennial's corporate wine buyer, discusses important wine buying tips as well as stories of his recent wine-buying trip to Australia. The podcast is now available for download from Centennial's web site, *www.centennialwines.com*. Moll also discusses everything from fine wine to backyard wines that go great with barbeque to wines in a box. He even discusses the importance of finding a consultant at a fine wine store to help match personal tastes with food rather than randomly picking wines off a shelf.
>
> Centennial, a Dallas-Fort Worth-based chain of 26 stores, sees podcasting as a great way to provide customers with helpful tips and interesting stories to make its wine experience more enjoyable, all at the consumer's convenience.

People love stories. They also want good, meaty information. Combining the two is vital, especially if your goods and services could be perceived as dry and boring. Find an angle to create human interest in your product. Go to Terry Brock's blog to hear his latest podcast at *http://yoursuccess.blogspot.com.*

Take a look at Dove's Real Beauty campaign. There are few things less intrinsically interesting than moisturizer. It's just a bunch of cold cream that sits in a jar until you slather it on your face. But Dove created an advertising campaign with a set of "real-life" models who were attractive if not super-model material. People identified with those models and wanted to find out more about them. They even showed up on Oprah and have been supported by an intensive web campaign. The consumer wants to know the Dove girls. She wants to hear their stories, so she sought them out. Sales of moisturizer rose as a result.

What storytelling opportunities exist with your products and services? Take some time to brainstorm ideas before you begin podcasting. Every field has potential to offer up great stories. A plumber can tell of some of the "nightmare" cases he's encountered. After all, who knows better what happens when a toddler shoves a teddy-bear down the toilet? A contractor can share details from the latest renovation project, providing armchair architects with insight from the front lines.

WHAT MAKES A GOOD PODCAST?

We've talked to small business owners who integrate podcasting into their marketing strategy. They agree that there are certain qualities that separate a good podcast from a bad one, and they were willing to share their insights. Here's what they had to say:

1. Craig Williams, of the Williams Law Firm, has a web site—*www.mayitpleasethecourt.com*—that features a blog and podcasts. It has resulted in well over $1,000,000 in referral business. Weekly podcasts feature pundits from opposite ends of the political spectrum discussing hot topics, current legal issues such as Supreme Court nominations and pending class action lawsuits. He says:

   • In Real Estate, they say "Location, Location, Location." In podcasting, it's "Content, Content, Content."

   • You have to be interesting. If you're not interesting, people won't listen.

   • Don't obsess over audible quality. You're not sending this to audiophiles who will be listening for every scratch and hiss. You're sending it to people who will be listening on an iPod or on their computer, where there's lots of distractions.

   • Speak clearly. You don't want to sound like you have marbles in your mouth.

   • The Internet is a great equalizer. You can be just as visible, have just as much of a presence, as companies that are much larger, much older, or have much deeper pockets.

2. Andy Wibbels, you met him in the blogging chapter, is an expert on blogging for business, has some great insights into podcasting. His web site is *www.andywibbels.com.* Here's what he's got to say:

    • Brevity is important, especially for a business podcast. Keep it concise, and get to the point fast.

    • Know your target audience, and how much time they have to listen to you. Do they have the time to listen to you for an hour every day, every week, twice a month?

    • Have realistic expectations about your podcasting schedule, and the time it takes to produce a podcast. It takes Wibbels 60 to 90 minutes to produce a half hour podcast. Don't overload your schedule.

    • Be consistent. If you promise a weekly podcast, deliver a weekly podcast.

PROMOTING YOUR PODCAST

If a podcast sits on an empty web site, does anyone hear it? You can put together the best podcast in the world, but if no one knows about it, you've just wasted a lot of time and energy.

Ways to promote your podcast include:

• Place a prominent link to your podcasts on your web site

• List your podcast on podcast directory sites. Some of these sites include:

  • *iPodder.org*

  • *PodcastAlley.com*

  • *PodcastingNews.com*

    Additionally, go to Google and type in *podcast* plus the name of your industry. You may find topical directories where tech-savvy searchers go to discover what podcasts are specifically geared toward their interest. Additionally, if you're an early adopter and come to podcasting sooner than others in your field, you'll have less competition.

When others jump on the podcasting bandwagon, you'll already be established as the oldest, most reputable podcast.

- Use podcast symbols to indicate where podcasts can be found on your company blog. Free to use symbols are available all over the web, including at many popular podcast directories.
- Consider putting links to your podcasts on your business cards, sales literature, and display materials.
- Submit your podcast to podcast review sites. Some of the best-known and most respected podcasting review sites are:

http://search.singingfish.com/sfw/submit.html
www.podcastalley.com/add_a_podcast.php
www.podcast.net/addpodcast
http://bloguniverse.com

THE SEVEN SCARY PODCASTING NO-NOS

Now that we've spent all this time telling you what to do during your podcast, you need to know that there are some things that you can't do. Some of these pitfalls will get you into trouble with the law, while others just make for bad listening. So watch out for:

1. *Copyrighted material.* We know you love that Journey song, and that you've played it every day since you started your

business back in 1983. You bought it on tape, you bought it on CD, you even have it on MP3. But guess what? You don't own the song. Playing it—or any other copyrighted performance—during your podcast is a definite no-no. There's a prevailing notion that if you only play a short segment—15 seconds or less—or that if you speak over the music, that you're not violating copyright. Sorry to tell you, but this prevailing notion is wrong. If you've just got to use a particular song, you'll need to secure permission from the artist and often his or her record label. Be prepared to pay big bucks, and kiss the idea of podcasts as a cost-effective promotional tool bye-bye! If you want music then go to *http://www.musicbakery.com,* where you can purchase royalty-free music from $19.99 to $39.99 that gives you the license to use the music when you want.

2. *Background noise.* The environment you record in has a big effect in the quality of your podcast. If you're recording at home or at the office, you run a risk of picking up a lot of ambient noise. Children playing, phones ringing, even a photocopier churning out reams of copies all come out loud and clear on your podcast—fatally damaging your professionalism.

3. *The Umma-uhhs.* No one speaks eloquently all the time. Even the most polished professional occasionally stumbles over a word. But listening to a three to five minute podcast filled with *Ummms* and *Uhhhs* and *You knows* is torture. Ask yourself how long you'd listen to someone else struggling to sort out his or her speech. The answer is probably not long. Luckily, the Umma-Uhhs are easily combated. Prepare your text before you start talking. Save the off-the-cuff speeches for after-dinner remarks.

4. *Statistics.* Numbers are the kiss of death. Sure, one or two snappy, attention grabbing facts—Did you know that 17 percent of all cab drivers wear green underwear on Fridays? It might work, but forget about communicating long columns of numbers, droning recitations of sales figures or complex calculations via podcast.

5. *Too much information (TMI).* The best podcasts are geared to the individual. It's one person talking to one person. Once you've done this once or twice, it's easy to feel very comfortable with the podcasting process. The whole thing has an intimate, conversational feel. The peril of this is that it is far too easy to reveal too much private or personal information—TMI. A good rule of thumb: If you wouldn't want your worst competitor to know that cute story about you, don't tell it.

6. *Badmouthing the competition.* There are two ways to get in trouble here. Obviously, you don't want to single out any of your competitors and highlight his or her failings in a forum as public as the Internet. You're liable to get slapped with a cease-and-desist order at best, a lawsuit at worst. Additionally, you're tarnishing your own reputation. Avoid the temptation, even when it's a general "Well, there are some people who do XYZ" type of comment.

7. *High-tech language.* Doctors, attorneys, accountants, and financial advisors, we're looking at you. Every profession has its own jargon, a series of industry-specific terms used to make communication among peers easier. However, this jargon is often unintelligible to the average layperson. Unless you're directing your podcast to a peer group, keep the jargon to a minimum. Explain unfamiliar terms,

and spell out abbreviations at least once. Remember, people won't appreciate what they don't understand!

HOW DOES IT WORK

The basic process to create a podcast involves four simple steps:

Step One: Design and create your content.
Step Two: Record your content in a digital format.
Step Three: Post your content to a webserver.
Step Four: Connect to an RSS feed.

There, that clears everything up, doesn't it? We've covered Step One pretty thoroughly, so let's skip to Step Two.

Step Two: Record Your Content in a Digital Format

Most podcasts are recorded in MP3 format (the MP3 is merely the most popular and prolific file format in use since digital music began to boom). This allows them to play as streaming media files and to be downloaded onto iPods and other popular digital media players.

To record your content as an MP3, you will need a microphone that plugs directly into your computer, a set of headphones, and some software. There are many types of free podcast creation programs available on the web. The most popular and user friendly include Audacity at *http://audacity.sourceforge.net* for use with both PCs and Macs and Garageband at *http://www.garageband.com,* currently only available for Macs. Easy podcast *http://www.easypodcast.com* is probably the simplest program available, with limited features but an appealing push-button operation.

Practice reading your text aloud once or twice before recording. Remember to speak slowly and clearly, without sounding abnormally stilted. You'll feel awkward at first, but practice makes perfect.

After your text is recorded, you can add background music or sound effects using a mixer. Remember, no copyrighted content! Choose from open source or creative commons material to protect your podcast. To use music effectively, consider using it at the beginning of the show, to mark segment changes throughout, and at the conclusion. Many listeners report a constant stream of background music to be distracting and annoying.

Step Three: Post Your Content to a Webserver

After you've created your podcast, you want to upload it to a webserver. This can be your blog, your web site, or a web site that you're affiliated with. Many of the podcasting creation programs automate this process for you, while others require you to send your content to a File Transfer Site (FTP site).

Unless you're a real tech-fanatic (and if you are, much of what you've read in this chapter is old, old news to you!) we recommend opting for an automated posting system. Most offer confirmation that you've successfully posted your podcast, making the process worry free.

Step Four: Connect to an RSS Feed

There are millions of individual web sites, blogs and even podcasts on the web. How will your target audience find you?

The best way is via an RSS feed. Remember, we talked about RSS feeds in the previous chapter. RSS feeds collect information from a multitude of web sites, and funnel it into programs called news aggregators. Common news aggregators are My Yahoo!, NewsGator, Net Newswire, and Sharp Reader. These programs let users know when new and interesting items go online. By using a catchy headline and a one- to two-sentence engaging description, you can entice new listeners to try out your podcast and let existing listeners know a new podcast is available.

WHAT KIND OF EQUIPMENT DO I NEED TO DO THIS MYSELF?

Podcasting can be as simple or as complex as you'd like it to be. It's possible to podcast from your cell phone or to record your shows in a professionally equipped studio. Obviously, better equipment allows higher-quality recording. This brings us to a pivotal point.

How good do your production values need to be?

This depends on your target audience. Will they expect a highly polished, broadcast-quality podcast, or will they be satisfied with something a little rougher around the edges?

Some qualities that are important to every audience:

- Clear delivery of content
- Minimal background noise
- Consistent audio levels

For the majority of small business owners, an acceptable quality level can be achieved with a minimal investment in equipment. The setup in Craig William's office—the one he uses to produce podcasts that bring in big-buck referrals—cost approximately $500.

The hardware you'll need, above and beyond your computer system, includes:

1. *Microphones.* If you're going to splurge on any aspect of podcasting, here's where you want to do it. The quality of your podcast depends on the quality of the original

recording. Luckily, this doesn't have to be very expensive. Good quality microphones begin around $100.

Take the time to try out different mikes and see how you sound before making a purchase. Not everyone sounds good on every microphone. For podcasting, you'll want to eliminate all background noise. For this reason, opt for a directional rather than stereo mike.

Avoid lapel microphones. They're not adequate for podcasting purposes.

2. *Headphones*. Wearing headphones allows you to monitor your podcast. You'll be able to hear what your broadcast sounds like before you post it to your web site. Select stereo headphones, and opt for a model that you'll be comfortable wearing for an hour at a time.

3. *Mixer*. Mixers are used to add additional audio tracks to your podcast and to record using more than one microphone. They're vital in maintaining a consistent audio level, preventing one speaker from being ear splittingly loud while another is barely audible.

When selecting mixers, shop with the following motto in mind: Maximum features for minimum price. As a base line, you want multiple audio inputs, three to four band equalizers, 10 channels with individually controlled audio levels, one master output, and one headset output. Prices for a bare-bones model will be in the low hundreds, and escalate heavenward as you get more sophisticated, powerful equipment.

Of course, audio equipment sales teams will sell you everything that you're willing to buy. It's possible to shell out thousands of dollars for voice brighteners, tone equalizers, bass dampeners, and a million other gadgets. Each has its place, and may be the right tool for a specific situation. But before you make the purchase, ask yourself, "Will this markedly improve the quality of my podcast? Do I need this to meet my target audience's expectations?"

THE TROUBLE WITH PODCASTING— AND HOPES FOR TOMORROW

Podcasting is a new technology. As such, there are still some bugs in the system. Early adopters and tech-savvy entrepreneurs have worked with and around these bugs, but that doesn't make them any less present. Currently, the main drawbacks to podcasting include:

1. *Hardware concerns.* Many small business owners don't currently have a microphone, mixer, and headphones on hand. These items need to be purchased, requiring a capital outlay, albeit a minimal one. Additionally, because you can always upgrade, there's the potential to get caught up buying more and more equipment to improve your production values.
2. *Office space.* Ideally, podcasts are recorded in an acoustically dead zone. Yet few of us select offices with an eye toward their potential as recording studios. Finding a quiet place to record your podcast can be troublesome.
3. *Software concerns.* Not all podcasting programs are as user-friendly as they could be. Adding music, sound effects, and other items to your recorded content can be time consuming, especially when you're new to podcasting.

Luckily, podcasting technology is evolving as quickly as the rest of the Internet. New software programs are being developed constantly, and existing programs are continually being improved. Podcasting is easier this year than it was last year, and next year, it will be even easier than it is now. On the consumer end, technology is evolving to make it easier to receive podcasts. You already see television shows available for download—and people watching them on their cell phones while riding the train to work!

VIDEO PODCASTING

Video podcasting has the potential to be an extremely valuable marketing tool for many small business owners. Imagine a custom-made TV show, centered around your business. The real estate agent's virtual tours could take on an additional dimension, with commentary from the homeowners, discussions of the neighborhood, or an interview with local schoolteachers, all available via cell phone, palm pilot, or laptop computer. Doctors could give a bird's eye view of common medical procedures, explaining common concerns to potential patients. The sky's the limit.

While audio podcasts are based on MP3 files, video podcasts are formatted as MOV files. Currently, the ease of production and posting that we see with audio podcasts does not exist in the video world. More equipment, expertise, and time are required. However, given the rapid advances we've seen surrounding audio podcasting, we wouldn't be surprised if video podcasting comes into its own within the next three to five years. It might be a good idea to start thinking about it now!

Chapter 11's Essential Essentials

1. Brainstorm stories to tell.
2. Link stories with great content about your service or product.
3. Buy the equipment.
4. Choose two or three podcast sites to list your podcast.
5. Review the Seven Scary Podcasting No-Nos.
6. Record your podcast—yes, you are ready.
7. Place your podcast on your web site or link to the podcast from your web site.
8. Connect your podcast to a couple of RSS feeds.

For more information on this topic, go to

www.essentialonlinesolution.com.

Step IV

Creating the Buzz
with Clicks and Clends

Chapter 12

Web Positioning

How Do They Find You?

Getting found by prospects who then turn into customers while you sleep is exhilarating. But how do you do that on the web?

Web positioning has become an art and a science that keeps on moving at lightning speed. We live in a world of Google this and that. We are constantly searching for one thing or another on the web but rarely look beyond the first 20 search results, yet there are thousands of choices. Coming up number one for a keyword is a market differentiator. This chapter explores the ins and outs of web positioning. It gives tips to make your site one that the search engines—and especially Google—ranks above your competitors'.

We must tell you right from the start that web positioning takes three to four months to make a difference. So start now. Don't wait.

HOW DOES A SEARCH ENGINE WORK?

It's a free service with computer generated search, called an *electronic spider*, which does not include any paid listings. Search engines are known for being an objective resource to get the information you want and need. Google is the number one search engine with 8 billion and counting web pages to check. When you conduct a search on Google, say, for "carpenters in Salt Lake City, Utah," a sponsored link appears in the top banner and in the right-hand column of the web page. These are paid ads to Google. But, no one pays to get ranked number one. Google does the ranking using some mysterious criteria. Did you know that Google supplies AOL, EarthLink, AT&T? So submitting to Google is worth your effort. If 55 percent of Internet users choose Google as their favorite search engine, it's a no-brainer to start here.

Search directories are a good place to also submit because they give you links and they help get you recognized by Google and other leading search engines.

WEB POSITIONING

Wow, your site is ranked #1 on Google, how'd you do that?

Anyone who has the bragging rights of being ranked in the top five for your service or product is always asked that question. Why? Because web positioning, which is where your web site places on search engines so buyers can find you, is critical to a successful online business.

Web positioning—or as it most often referred to as *Search Engine Optimization* (SEO)—is definitely an art and science. It's an art because the rules are constantly changing. You need to imagine sometimes what is needed to rank high. It is also a science because search engines and most directories use electronic spiders to reach out to the billions of web pages and conduct an algorithm to decide which should be ranked. Why all the rule changes? When techies or web site owners have figured out the "formula," or close to it to be constantly highly ranked, they can begin to manipulate the rankings. To deter manipulation and be a free, open, objective source, search engines are always changing the requirements to keep everyone on their toes and honest. The search engines want that level playing field as much as possible so they can be seen and valued as an objective source of information. That sounds good to us small business owners.

In this chapter, we are going to look at how to position your web site to stand out in the SEO war. As we stated, this information changes rapidly so we'll give you sources to keep up to date. In addition, we'll tackle this question: Do SEO yourself, or hire a company? It's an important question with SEO.

Importance of High-Ranking Web Site

Why is it important to be on the first page of a search engine or directory? Okay, be honest, how many times have you gone beyond the first page of web sties when you're looking for something on the web on, say, Google? We bet you can count that on one hand. Why? Most visitors are impatient browsers. They want the information quickly, and let's face it; if a site is on the first page it must be good. Right?

The saying is, "If you're not in the top 20, forget it."

Getting on the first page results from having a web site that corners keywords or phrases so that they always come up when entered, when they are "owned" so to speak.

What Do Small Business Owners Say about SEO?

All the small business people that we've interviewed have said empathically *yes*; you must optimize your web site. But they've also said it is hard work and takes time. Read what a couple of business owners told us.

Steve Waterhouse, CSP, sales training consultant and author—*www.waterhousegroup.com*—provided this list:

- Don't trust your web designer to be an SEO expert.
- Some SEO companies use technologies that will get you banned from Google. If the technique sounds improper to you, it does to Google, too.
- Friends matter: make sure you exchange links with everyone who has a relevant site to maximize your ranking.
- Nothing is more powerful that a page-one ranking on Google (we are #5). It drives business to us daily.
- Changes happen daily. Find an expert who keeps up and works with them.

Chris Gatti, owner of CRG Associates, a training and development firm—*www.crgassocs.com*—told us:

- Know the "rules" for SEO change constantly.
- Being optimized once doesn't guarantee ongoing optimization.
- Use a service that is current on this fast-changing area so that you don't make big errors on your own.
- Do it!! It makes a difference!

Steve White of Growth Communications, a web designer who also does SEO—*www.growthcommunications.com*—says:

- Pick proper keyword phrases.
- Check the keyword density on each web page.
- Get links to your site and within your site. Don't link unless it's of value to you.
- Think budget—if you can afford to only do SEO halfway, that's like doing nothing at all. (However, other experts

disagree and believe that SEO is something that can be done on a gradual basis.)
- Write articles.

Should I Even Attempt to Do SEO?

Wow, you might be asking yourself, "Should I even attempt to do anything myself?" Yes!

Mary Sandro, owner of ProEdge Skills, a customer service and presentation skills company—*www.proedgeskills.com*—is rated #1 for customer service and presentation skills. She is adamant that, as a small business owner, you should know how SEO operates and then decide if you want to do it on your own. But as a small business person you need to know the ins and outs of SEO so you won't get taken for a hefty, expensive ride.

Make Sure You Track Results!

Before you begin, make sure you track where your traffic is coming from if you already have a site. If you are building a new site, start tracking right from the beginning. This way you will know what is working and where you are drawing traffic from.

What Are the Elements of Web Positioning?

Figure 12.1 shows the areas to consider. There are a couple more areas you could look at like page ranking, but we are going to focus on the top three to get you started.

Figure 12.1 Elements of Web Positioning

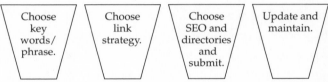

What's the Cost?

The cost for SEO depends on whether you do your search engine optimization yourself or buy resources to do it for you. Mary Sandro of Pro Edge Skills states, "You always pay one way or the other." It's a pure and simple business decision. When Mary started out positioning her web site six years ago, she did all the research and work herself. She thinks that today, with all the rapid changes, you need to know how to optimize your site but not necessarily do it yourself. As a business owner you want to know what SEO entails so you don't get ripped off by someone who says they know what they are doing.

Do it yourself means you want to buy some software tools and you must submit your site to Yahoo!, which charges for submission. So figure with tools and the like around $500. To buy resources, the price can range from $1,500 for review of your site with recommendations for you to implement or hire someone to $1,000 or more a month. The range obviously runs from the basics to every day attention to your web site. Let's get serious here. When you are first starting out with SEO, unless you have deep pockets—if you did you wouldn't have read this far in the book— we would suggest you do most of this yourself. If you can afford to do so, search for a reputable SEO small firm and have it do a review with recommendations. Then you can make a decision as to what you can afford to do yourself with your limited time or what you can afford to pay someone to do.

KEYWORDS AND PHRASES

Have you been wondering, "What's the scoop on keywords? I heard they were passé now." Of course, some of you have, and for good reason. Keywords used to be the most important SEO tool. Nowadays they are not a driving force in SEO; but search engines do pay attention to them. It is important for you to spend the time discovering which keyword phrases people are typing in to Google and other search engines to help pinpoint the right words for you.

How Do I Determine My Keyword Phrases?

1. *How many keywords should I have?* According to Andy Komack of KoMarketing, a SEO firm—*www.komarketingassociates. com*—going after one keyword makes it very difficult to get your site ranked in the top five web sites on a page. Three words are reasonable and four words done right should help get you there. For Andy, with his company doing the SEO, the site should get to #1 he told us. Of course, we were drooling.

2. *Think about how people will search for you.* What will your potential customer be looking for? A local electrician? A store that sells dyed shoes? Wouldn't you be shocked if the words you choose to be found were words that no one or very few people actually search for? What a waste of your time and money to position your web pages for something that no one will be finding. Ouch! To prevent this from happening to you take a couple of the words you think people put in Google to find you and do these exercises.

Exercise One: Use Yahoo!'s Search Marketing Tools

The best place to get started demystifying the whole topic of keywords and pay per click advertising is *www.overture.com*. When you visit the Overture site (now owned by Yahoo!) you will first see a page titled "Yahoo! Search Marketing". Click on Visit Resource Center. There you can see some easy to understand explanations of various keywords. But, the key element on this page is in a section called Tools. The first tool is called a Keyword Selector Tool. When you open it, it allows you to type in various words or phrases that you think people would use in searching for your site. It will also give you the statistics of how many times someone typed in the term that you are researching. You will learn that certain phrases are more popular than others. For example, the term *gift store* was searched 15,000 times in April 2006, but the term *gift shops* was searched over 35,000 times in the same month.

What does it all mean? In building your site, include the most popular search terms. This will ensure that more people will find your site. This tool will also help you know what words you should consider in any of your pay-per-click advertising campaigns.

Yahoo! Search Marketing also has tutorials that contain excellent tips on ways to optimize your search marketing. You may also want to check out the calculators.

Exercise Two: Use Google Adwords

A second source for determining which words and phrases are best for your business is *http://adwords.google.com*. Under the Learn More section, click on Explore search queries. In the Keyword Variations tab you are asked to enter a keyword or phrase, and then search for Keyword popularity. (You do have other choices here, such as Keywords, Cost and ad position estimates, Global search trends, and Negative keywords. Experiment with the different categories. But for now, we are just going to focus on Keyword popularity.)

Once you have typed in your keyword, click on Get More Keywords. You will see a list of similar words and their popularity.

You will notice three columns. The first column shows the amount of advertiser competition. The second column shows the phrase's search volume. The third column shows the type of match you want. Broad, Phrase, or Exact. We generally like to do broad searches but try all the different types. You will soon discover one of the secrets of search marketing. You will see words or phrases that have very heavy advertiser competition but with low search volume. Why? It happens because businesses see what words their competition use and feel an obligation to jump on the empty bandwagon. It happens to all of us. It is as if to say our competition must know something we don't know. Go where there is some traffic.

Before you leave Google Adwords, explore the Adwords Help Center. It will walk you through various terms and formulas to use. Adwords promises to get you customers in 15 minutes and they mean it. This is a powerful tool to help you not only select the words or phrases to incorporate in your site, but also help you to select the words to use in a pay-per-click campaign.

Exercise Three Wordtracker

Wordtracker, *www.wordtracker.com,* is what the pros use to determine what words or phrases to use. It is a paid service, but does allow one free trial. You can buy a subscription for day, a week, a month, or a year, with prices starting at $7.91 for a day, all the way up to $263.51 for a year. As it says on its home page, "Amateurs guess. Professionals know." The reason to use Wordtracker is that it combines all searches, not just Google or Yahoo!. Google and Yahoo! are great indicators, but Wordtracker is more conclusive.

Take the Wordtracker tutorial and try the free trial. Then purchase the service as you need it. A week here or there. Use it to brainstorm new terms to use. But there is a word of warning: Be careful in selecting words or phrases that are drawing over 500,000 hits. You can get lost in the competition and pay high rates for pay-per-click advertising. And, while you may draw traffic to your site, those visiting may not be serious buyers. We are living in a world of specialists and that's what keyword searches are all about. Find your niche and you'll get rich.

(It is recommended that you download your searches into a Word or Excel document so that you can compare and track them. All of these services allow for that, and it's a pretty good way to keep track of them rather than constantly writing them down.)

Exercise Four: Choose Your Keywords Phrase

Review all three sources of keywords and phrases and choose the three or four word keyword phrase for your web site. We know it's hard to choose one keyword phrase. Use your data as your guiding light in this effort. Then go for it.

What Do I Do with the Keyword Phrase I Decided On?

Take your fabulous keyword phrase. (Barbara's is "leadership development consultant.") It is fabulous, isn't it? It's your work that you're doing and you want to attract more of this type of work. Right?

Go to your web site and make sure that your keyword phrase is in these areas:

1. *Title tags*. The blue bar on top of the page
    Make sure that your home page title bar *does not say* Home and then your web site name—for example, Home, *Leadership, Callan Consulting*. Barbara's Home Page Title tag is *Leadership Development Consultant, Barbara Callan-Bogia*. Rick's is *Rick Segel, Retail Sales Training, Retail Marketing Consultant, Retail Mentor and Speaker*. What's yours say?
2. *Headers of pages*. Need to be H1 tags (this is html speak) with your keyword phrases

3. *Subheader*. Make H2 tags
4. *Bold text*. To make a strong tag

Coding HTML

When Barbara went to change her headers on her pages to H1 tags, she didn't realize that she needed to enter the information in the HTML section of her Content Management system. So guess what she had on her front page of her web site? <h1>Leadership Consulting</h1>. How embarrassing! So she quickly called her web person to discover that she needed to switch to the HTML program on the Content Management site to enter the H1 tags. So know where to code HTML on your site or have your web person do it. Mary Sandro of ProEdge Skills recommends:

- *Webpositon—www.webposition.com—is a good product to use that teaches you to design pages so that the keywords are used properly and in the correct places.*
- *The title tag is the most important. Be sure it contains keywords. Be sure it is the first in the html.*
- *Use keywords in Headers, Links, and body text.*
- *Use keywords in alt text behind images.*

Keyword Density

Content rich web copy is crucial for your site. And the number of times you use your keyword phrase or phrases helps the search engines determine what you site is about.

According to the folks at The Internet Marketing Center—*www.marketingtips.com*—in Corey Rudl's *The Insider Secrets to Marketing Your Business on the Internet, Version 2005*, keyword density equals the total number of times the keyword appears, divided by the total number of works, multiplied by 100. So what does that mean? Let's take an example of the keyword "retail" and our sentence is "Retail is my life." In this case, the keyword density of "retail" would be 25 percent. *Retail* is used once in the four-word sentence, which is good. You do not want to overload your web page with your keywords. This called "stuffing" and the search engines will penalize you for this or even ban you. Don't even think of going there.

Every web page on your site should have your keyword phrases on them. Write the web page copy so that your customer will like it and it accomplishes your keyword density strategy.

Keyword phrases are important to help search engine spiders verify that your content and site tags are aligned. Besides if you design your keyword phrase for your prospective customers they will find you. Isn't that what all this time and effort is all about anyway?

Chose Your Link Strategy

You're probably thinking, "What's a link and why do I need it?" Keywords should get me seen by Google. That kind of thinking will get you in trouble. As we've stated, the web is always changing and in the last two years links have grown in importance to Google—so everyone needs to pay attention.

There are two kinds of links: incoming and outgoing. The incoming links are ones about which people say, "Hey, that's a great site. I want to link to it. I want to go to that site with just a click." These are the "good" links for web positioning. How many incoming links should your web site have?

Great question.

According to *Search Engine News*, a good number to aim for is a minimum of 50 incoming links. External links, however, won't do you much good. You place links on your site to send people someplace else. Why would you do that? Don't you want people to stay on your site and—more importantly—be seen by Google as the "go to" web site for your particular industry, knowledge, and product?

Okay, now that we know we want incoming links—links coming into us—you're thinking, how do I get those links?

In "A Four Step Plan for Getting Started with Links...The Ultimate Link Building Quick-Start Guide," Esoos Bobnar of *SearchEngineNews.com* makes a case for a four-step process for incoming links. Step 1 is to submit your site to the top directories; Step 2 to target article directories; Step 3 is to write and distribute a few press releases; and Step 4 is to buy some links.

We are not crazy about buying links until or unless you *really* know what you are doing on the web. A good portion the Bobnar article is devoted to telling how to watch out when buying links. It's only for the daredevils and those who are okay with a lot of risk. In case you didn't know, you could get banned from Google and other search engines and directories for purchasing links. It's called a *link farm*. Don't do it.

There are many sources on the web to find information about link strategies. Just be careful. We recommend that you start out with this approach and then build on it.

1. *Write and submit articles.* Writing great articles positions you as an expert, the go-to person, and builds your credibility. Include in your byline a link to your site so that readers can find you to see what else you have written or offer.

   Submit the free articles to article directories. One of the directories you can start with is *GoArticles.com.*

In Googling "submit article for free," we got 72,700 results, so you can do the same and see where it makes sense to submit your articles. It's a great method to get your name and ideas out in cyberspace and spread your links. Also, try Googling for article directories in your topic or industry area.

How many articles should you write? We recommend that you submit at least one article every month. If you are not a writer or don't have time, find someone at *Elance.com* or *CraigLists.com* to ghostwrite the article for you. Just make sure that you are specific that the work is fee based and no royalties come out of the work. This is a work-for-hire situation.

2. *Check out your links.* Use either or both of these free link services to discover who is linking to your site.

   • *LinkPopularity.com*
   • Link Analysis—*http://www.seotoolset.com/tools/free_tools.html#linkanalysis*

   You can also check out who is linking to your competition. If certain vendors and others you know could link to your site, invite them to do so.

3. *Check out your broken links.* You know when you have a bulb out in your neon sign or the outgoing message on your voicemail is not the right date. So how do you know if you have broken links on your web site? Lucky for us there are places on the web that will notify you of your broken links.

   Two places that have a free trial for you to try out are:

   • *SEVENtwentyfour.com*
   • *LinkAlarm.com*

When Barbara first used *SEVENtwentyfour.com*, she found out that her *info@callanconsulting.com* link, which was at the bottom of every page, was broken! Imagine how quickly she got that fixed.

4. *Build a site map.* Imagine taking a trip to Paris and not having a map with you to find your way around. Scary isn't it? A web site map helps your visitors find their way around your web site, especially if you have a lot of pages. More importantly a site map that is linked to every page on your site gives you internal links. And guess what? Search engines love site maps. It's easier for the electronic spider to search the web pages. So make sure you have a site map that is linked to each of your web pages.

Chose and Submit Your Site to Search Engines and Directories

Who should you submit your web site to? Submit first to the free ones, of course, and then pay to submit to Yahoo!. You do not want to submit to more than three a week. If you do, the search engines will pick up on that and think you are overdoing links. So, steady submitting rather than a blast is best.

Should you submit your site manually or hire a service to submit your site?

You should submit your web site manually to each of the search engines and directories. Of course, you could hire a teenager to do this, but you do not want or need to hire a service to submit your site. It's not a good use of your money. And some web submission sites are not reputable and you can experience problems.

Chose Search Engines and Directories

To start, submit to the search engines and directories shown in Table 12.1.

Table 12.1 Top Search Engines and Directories

Search Engines

---

*Google.com—http://www.google.com/intl/en/submit_
content.html*

*MSN.com—10 percent of Internet users use it—
http://search.msn.com/docs/submit.aspx*

Directories

Yahoo!—costs $299 a year—http://yahoo.com

Open Directory—http://dmoz.org/add.html

What other directories should I submit my web site to?

You should look for directories in the industry associations you belong to. One of the most underutilized directories is Yahoo!'s Yellow Pages—*http://yp.yahoo.com*. You can be listed on the site for free; but you can also be a sponsored advertiser in the yellow pages. There are currently three advertising tiers. Check them out to see if any of these tiers would work well for your local business.

How Do I Submit My Site?

Only submit your site to the search engines and directories when you've got your keyword and phrases along with your links ready.

All set? Good. If you want to check if there have been any changes since we went to press, check these resources for up-to-date information:

- *SearchEngineWatch.com*

- *SearchEngineNews.com*—$97 subscription—but you can find information there to alert you to new updates in the industry

Go to each search engine or directory web site that you want to submit and find the submission page. See the above URL addresses to submit to the search engines and directories we recommended and take it from there.

Update and Maintain Your Site

Here's the real test of commitment to online success—updating your site on a regular basis. You knew this was coming, didn't you? If your web site is not updated on a regular basis, then the search engines view this site as a dormant site because there is nothing new to add so they stop searching your site. We can get caught up in building the most beautiful site, and you think that's it. You're done. Your web site is up and you have your keyword phrases implanted into the content-rich copy on the site. But if you don't regularly add articles or change some items for sale and so on, the web site is just a brochure that people who know you can go to look at; no one is searching and finding you with type of site. Correct?

Maintenance requires that you stay on top of any broken links that might occur on your site. Remember, we like and the search engines like internal links so make sure they aren't broken. Change your copy if you change what you really focus on as businessperson.

Maintain your site so that is up to date with the latest in web positioning techniques. If not, your site, which you have built to attain first-page rankings, could slip into the black hole of cyberspace.

Chapter 12's Essential Essentials

1. Choose your keyword phrase.
2. Make sure your web site content is rich in your keywords. Check out your keyword density factor.
3. Load your title, header, and subheaders tags with your keyword phrase.
4. Write and submit articles to gain organically grown links.
5. Submit to the key search engines and directories.
6. Remember it takes three to fourth months to see a difference; but track to make sure your web positioning has made a difference in your hits and conversions to sales.

For more information on this topic, go to

www.essentialonlinesolution.com.

Chapter 13

Pay Per Click:
A.K.A. Pay for Performance

A New Way to Advertise

Pay per click has revolutionized marketing forever. Due to the increasing number of web sites and the difficulty of getting on the top 10 of any search engine, a simple idea became a goliath industry. If you can't make it to the top, buy your way there.

Learn the secrets of this new marketing tool because it can be dangerous if you don't. Did we get your attention with that? Good, because we don't want you to skim through this chapter. Read and reread this chapter before you start a pay per click campaign. You'll thank us that you did.

Simply stated, pay per click marketing consists of placing an ad in a pay per click search engine and then paying each time a person clicks on that ad. You've seen these ads on the right-hand column of the search results pages for Google and Yahoo! to name a few, and on the top of other pages. If your ad is not clicked, then you don't pay. Now some search engines penalize you for not being clicked, such as Google, so they can and will put your ad on hold or disable it. Other search engines have a monthly spend minimum.

The beauty of online advertisement is that you have the opportunity to test an ad and make changes on the fly, which you certainly can't do if you placed a print ad in a business journal for six months.

The best part about online marketing is that your ad will send highly targeted and predictable traffic to your site. This reason alone should increase your sales.

Another way to look at pay per click online marketing is that once you have positioned your web site with your title tags and keywords, and so on, you also show that you own that space for the keyword phrase and you have an ad to let people know about you.

Pay per Click Vocabulary You Should Know

The pay per click (PPC) industry is just like any other in that they have their own terms for what they do. Here are a few critical terms that you need to know for a successful ad campaign:

- *Clickthrough rate (CTR).* The number of visitors that actually click on your ad divided by the number of times your ad appears.
- *Impressions.* The number of times your ad appears.
- *Unique visitors.* The number of individuals who visit your site for the first time.
- *Cost per click (CPC).* Cost to you everytime someone clicks on your ad.
- *Cost per acquisition.* Money spent to get the sale, lead, subscription, and so on.

Should You Run a Pay per Click Campaign?

Running a pay per click campaign can turn out to be the best and most lucrative online advertising you can do for your company or the most expensive drain on your company's cash flow. Take, for instance, the small businessperson who told us that he spends over $300 a month on his pay per click campaign and thinks that's okay, while another online advertiser spends about $25 a month on his PPC campaign and is getting great results. What makes the difference? The difference is how much each person was willing to spend on keywords. As you can imagine, one person was spending over $1 a keyword while the other person was spending less than 25 cents a word. Big difference.

Okay, so what are the advantages of running a pay per click campaign?

- More cash in less time
- Increased customer traffic to your web site
- More targeted prospects to your web site
- Quick way to reach new customers

Just remember that *caution* is the watchword in any advertising adventure. Check and make sure that a pay per click initiative fits your company's business model. There's not much sense in doing a pay per click campaign when all of your work is generated by referrals from your BNI group or you are financially cash flow poor. That said, online marketing is the new and here-to-stay model that most businesses will be using. Isn't that why you are reading this book? We thought so.

HOW DOES A PAY PER CLICK CAMPAIGN WORK?

The process of creating and managing a pay per click campaign is shown in Figure 13.1 and follows these steps:

Figure 13.1   Pay per Click Campaign

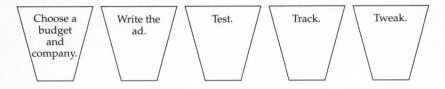

1. Choose your budget and ad company.
2. Write the ad.
3. Test your ad.
4. Track results.
5. Tweak to keep the money rolling in.

Choose a Budget and a Search Engine Pay per Click Company

Determining advertising budgets is one of the most difficult things to do when you are just getting started. The reason for this is, if your ad works, you end up spending a smaller percentage of sales than you planned. But if your ad doesn't work, you will spend more. Having said that, pay per click programs make advertising budgeting a little bit easier because eventually you are able to determine the advertising costs per sale (which mass media advertising can't tell you).

The best way to begin is to simply determine how much money you can afford to spend without any return at all. Treat pay per click advertising as if it were image advertising or research, because it is a combination of both. Understand that the goal in pay per click advertising is to create an ad that people will click on, taking them to your site, and selling them something.

In planning your pay per click advertising program, here are the questions to answer:

1. **How much does it cost for every impression of your ad (cost per impression)?**

   It is important to understand that impressions in pay per click advertising are theoretically free. You only pay when someone clicks on your site. In banner advertising however, you are paying for every impression. But, if you select keywords that are extremely popular and lots of people click through and don't buy anything, it's quite expensive. That is why you want to be careful with the terms you select. The terms should be broad enough to mean something to your potential customers, but narrow enough for your ads to be effective, attracting the customers that would be more likely to buy something.

2. **How many impressions does it take to have someone click through to my site (known as the click-through rate), and how do you calculate the click-through rate?**

   This varies by industry, product, and most importantly, the strength of the ad. You can calculate your CTR (click-through rate) by dividing the number of times a phrase is searched by the number of time people click through to your site. So, for example, is a phrase is searched 1000 times a month and 50 people click through. That is a 5 percent CTR.

3. **What is the cost per click?**

   The cost per click is how much the word or phrase costs each time it was clicked on. This price is determined before you begin in the bidding process for various terms.

4. **How many click throughs does it take to convert into a sale?**

   Known as the conversion rate percentage, this is calculated by dividing the number of click throughs by the amount of sales. You can calculate this per day, per week, per month, per quarter, per year. It's up to you. For example: If 50 people clicked through in a day and five of those people bought something, your conversion rate for the day would be 10 percent.

5. **What is your acquisition cost per sale?**

The acquisition cost per sale is the dollar amount you paid per click (as discussed in question three) divided by the number of sales you made. So, for example, if you paid $1 per click, attracted 50 people to your site, and made five sales, your acquisition cost would be:

50 people who visited your site × $1.00 paid per click ÷ 5 sales.

So, the acquisition cost each sale in this example is $10.00 per sale.

6. **What is the profit per sale?**

You know what the product costs are and how much it costs to acquire that sale. So what remains is the gross profit per sale. If you sell a gift at $50.00 and the product cost is $25.00 and the acquisition cost is $10.00, your gross profit per click is $15.00.

Now you must determine what other expenses should be included in that sale. Once you know all of these numbers, budgeting becomes a snap. Actually it almost eliminates the need for budgeting. As long as you can produce the product, ship it in a timely manner, and show a profit per piece, who cares what the budget is?

Which Company to Choose?

You mean I have a choice as to which company I want to run my ad campaign? We know you thought it was only Google AdWords, right? Actually, there are many pay per click search engines.

Google and Yahoo! (which now owns Overture) are among the top along with several others. Overture was the company that really put pay per click on the map of Internet marketing.

Review the way each search engine places a pay per click ad. You may want to start with a smaller search engine and move up to the big players—or start right away with the big boys. It's up to your business model, your budget, and how confident you are in your ad copy and customer identification.

When choosing a pay per click search engine keep in mind:

- Will you do the ad campaign yourself or get help?
- Will you want to pay the search engine for help or get a techie to do it?
- Do you want instant ad placement or are you willing to wait a few days to a week?
- Where (search engines) do you want your ads to appear online?
- Which budget feature will work best with your advertising model?
- What's your overall ROI for online marketing?
- Are you willing to keep, track, and test your ads on a regular basis?

Check out these sites to keep up with the latest changes in the pay per click marketing world:

- *PayPerClickGuru.com*
- *PayPerClickAnalyst.com/*

A Review of the Top Pay per Click Search Engines

We've reviewed two of the top pay per click search engines to give you a sense of what each one offers. Whichever one you choose, you must follow its guidelines.

GOOGLE ADWORDS™—HTTPS://ADWORDS.GOOGLE.COM

Google is the place to be. It boasts an 80 percent reach to Internet users for its online advertising network. When you conduct an online ad campaign with Google, you place the ad in its network, which includes AOL, Jeeves, AT&T Network, EarthLink, and more. Not bad company to be seen in.

According to a Google guru Andrew Goodman, "Google AdWords is the largest advertising opportunity on the Internet today, bar none. Google will make more than $5 billion this year from the program."

So what other reasons are there to use Google and make money?

Pro

1. It's quick to get up and running. Twenty minutes or less.
2. It's inexpensive to get started. Only $5 and a minimum cost-per-click from one cent to $100.
3. Set a daily budget for spending on your account.
4. You only pay a penny more than your competitor.
5. The more effective your ad is, the less you pay to maintain its ranking.
6. You can run multiple ads for each keyword so you can test several ads simultaneously to see which one is a moneymaker.
7. Google has a learning center to help get you started—*http://www.google.com/adwords/learningcenter.*

Con

1. Google determines the advertising ranking of its AdWords by a combination of ad performance (click-through rate) and the amount an advertiser agrees to pay per click.

2. This means that if your ad is not pulling enough traffic, your bid could end up in an inactive state or not show up at all. So always track your ad activity.
3. You do not know what your competition is bidding.

Once you get savvy, you can use other kinds of ads as well. There are site-targeted ads; broad match, phrase match, exact match, and use of negative keywords (identify keywords you don't want your ad to appear with—such as *toddler* with day care when you want *dog* plus day care.

Pay per Click U

Check out Google Adwords guru Perry Marshall's free five-day e-mail course at www.perrymarshall.com/google.

Yahoo! Search Marketing—
http://searchmarketing.yahoo.com
Notice that Yahoo!'s pay per click campaign does not use the same terms. It calls the same process *Search Marketing*. When you use Yahoo! Search Marketing, your ads could land on Yahoo!, AltaVista, *CNN.com*, *MSN.com* (It is its own site supposed to be breaking away in 2006), and *Infospace.com*. These are accessed by up to 90 percent of the active Internet users. Good places for your ad to be seen, don't you think?

Pro

1. Overture, which Yahoo! bought in 2005, was the tool to use in the beginning of online advertising.
2. Has two programs to choose from: Self-Service and FastTrack.

3. You can see what other people are bidding on keywords.

This can be a pro or a con depending on how you look at it: You can pay to be first and own the keyword or you must pay a higher fee even if your ad has a good CTR.

Con

1. $30 initial deposit is nonrefundable but will be applied to click throughs or to the minimum monthly spend
2. $20 minimum monthly spend

In addition to the previous considerations, Yahoo! Search Marketing offers include:

- *Self Service for no service fee* (you still have a nonrefundable initial deposit fee of $30). Yup, you do everything on your own in setting up your pay per click ad campaign. Your ad campaign is subject to review before your ad is approved. This can take some time.
- *Fast Track.* For a $199 service fee, unless you find a discount like we did, the Fast Track package can get you up and running sooner. It features assistance on search term selections, titles and descriptions, budget and strategy advice, a proposal, along with tracking assistance of the URLs. In addition, your site review is included and takes less time. Of course, you are paying for this help.

If you search for *Yahoo! Search Marketing* with a search engine, and look at the ads on the right-hand column, you may find a discount campaign for Yahoo! Search Marketing that will save you money on your first campaign. Give it a try. Right now there is a site offering $50 off either the Self-Serve package or the Fast Track package. What's the difference between the two Yahoo! Search

Marketing offerings? Money and whether you want help to get you started.

Yahoo! also offers Local Sponsored Searches that have no monthly minimum. This would be good for plumbers, electricians, woodworkers, and other tradespeople and smaller business entrepreneurs. Other pay per click search engines are shown in Table 13.2.

Table 13.2   Other Pay Per Click Search Engines

Miva.com	*Looksmart.com*
Search123.com	*ePilot.com*
Blowsearch.com	*Mamma.com*
Enhance.com	*Searchfeed.com*
Kanoodle.com	*Business.com*

As we are writing this Microsoft Corporation is preparing MSN® adCenter, its new pay per click program. Stay tuned and check it out at *http://advertising.msn.com/home.*

Write Your Ad

Copy, as we have been saying throughout this book, makes the difference of an ad being read and acted upon. Look again at the chapters on web copy and keywords for web positioning. If you haven't done the work in the previous chapters, you may want to stop and do that work now. If you think a pay per click campaign will be the marketing silver bullet for your business, think again. There have been many online marketers who placed all of their business in one basket—an online marketing campaign—and woke up one morning with a well gone dry. Why? Because one of the search engines decided to change the rules. So don't just pursue one online business solution initiative. It's like the consultant who has all his or her work with one client and then the client no longer needs or wants the consultant's services. So the consultant has no work having never marketed the business to anyone else. Enough said.

Before You Begin Writing

Do what you do now. Check what ads your competition has on the Internet. Check how many ads there are in your space. Perry Marshall, the Google guru, states:

> Before I start a Google campaign, I take a look to find out how many bidders are bidding on my keyword. If there's less than 10, it's going to be a day at the beach. More than 30, we'd better sharpen our pencils. More than 60: only experienced web marketers should play.

When we checked who was advertising leadership development training, there were over 85 ads for that space. Wow! Those are not good odds. Back to the drawing board for that campaign.

Another thing to consider is what web page you are going to have the ad linked to at your business web site. In other words, where will your prospective customer land? On the home page? On the page that sells what you are advertising? Keep in mind Google looks for relevant match ads. Does the ad take you the customer to a place that matches the ad? Or is the ad a come-on? If it's not a match, you're in trouble.

What makes a good ad campaign copy?

1. *Titles*
   - Keywords in the headlines
   - Grab attention

2. *Content*

- Address how your product or service will make life easier or solve a problem.
- Use the words *free, instant or bonus.*
- Bold keywords—but don't overdue it.
- Use a Call to Action. These are words that motivate your customers to purchase and item or contact you. Some examples are "Join Now," "Subscribe," "Make," and "Get."

3. *Web site address (URL)*

- Bold some of the web site name.
- The web site address relates to the copy or topic.

Each pay per click search engine site has its own guidelines so check them out as you begin your writing session. How many words can you have in the title, the content, and the like?

More than One Ad Is a Good Thing

As you write your ad copy know the keywords that you want to test. Have several different ones ready to begin testing.

Testing the Ad Campaign

Congratulations! You have your ad copy ready. You have submitted your ad to the search engine. You probably want to submit a second ad that you run simultaneously to test a keyword phrase. Only change one thing about the ad so you can test almost apples to apples. Maybe you change the title so the content is the same but one word in the title of the ad is different. Or you change a word in the copy or offer a different item or free item. You get the idea.

Tracking the Ad Campaign

Now watch what happens. Track the results so you know exactly where your traffic is coming from and which ad is pulling in what kind of traffic. See which ad you get the best results from. Which ad are you getting hits on? Which ad is pulling in the sales? Which ad is drawing traffic that stays on your web site longer? Again, go back to what was your objective in the first place in running a pay per click ad campaign. Is that objective being realized?

How to Get Web Statistics

Your web person or service can provide the statistical data to you. They can generate stats for keywords that people used to find your site, how long they stay on your site, which pages they click to on your site, how they came to your site, and so on. Amazing information.

Keep testing your ads and the results you are getting. If you like the results, just keep monitoring the statistics. If you are not happy with the results then change the ad to bring you the results you want.

Tweaking the Ad Campaign

With all the fast changes on the Internet, sitting back and thinking your online ad campaign is set once you begin to get the results you want is a fallacy. Remember the businesspeople we wrote about in the beginning of the chapter? You know the ones, who only had online marketing as their business presence? Well, this is why you need to continually tweak your ad or ads. The rules keep changing. You need to keep up with them and keep fresh. Here's one example. For a financial planner, long-term care is the hot item one year—and then the next year it's baby boomer retirement planning. You need to stay on top of what you place in your ads to reflect what your customer wants that you have to sell to them.

Chapter 13's Essential Essentials

1. Define the objectives you intend to achieve by running a pay per click ad campaign.
2. Decide your budget for the ad campaign aiming for the second to fourth spots.
3. Choose the pay per click search engine that best fits your business needs.
4. Write the ad copy.
5. Test two or three ads at the same time to know which ad is best.
6. Track the ad statistics to know the impact of your ad on your business.
7. Tweak the ad to ensure that you stay in the number two or three spot.
8. Stay current with the changes that take place on a regular basis in the pay per click advertising world. Tweak or change your ad to reflect these new changes so you stay in place.

For more information on this topic, go to

www.essentialonlinesolution.com.

Chapter 14

Advertising

Traditional and Nontraditional

The issue we debated most in writing this book was whether traditional forms of advertising should be included. One side of the argument was that because this book focuses on the "online solution" then the answer must be to focus on the nontraditional, online advertising. The other side of the argument was that just because the business is online doesn't mean the advertising must be online. After all, Monster and Go Daddy had significant increases in business with their Super Bowl ads. Amazon and eBay are certainly not strangers to traditional forms of marketing either.

Zappos, the online shoe retailer, bucked all of the odds when it adopted a newspaper advertising policy. Most traditional merchants have been disappointed with newspaper advertising results—but Zappos, an online merchant, built a substantial business using this medium. The goal is reaching your potential customer so that you can do more business with them. Rick and his wife Margie make most of their purchases online, including all of their apparel. When Margie placed an order at Zappos online, she found the perfect pair of shoes without looking at anything but the Zappos web site. However, almost simultaneously, Rick found a Zappos ad in *USA Today* and placed his order on the basis of that ad. Both husband and wife did the same business but in one of these purchases a traditional print ad factored. Don't give up on all of the traditional sources.

Also, the integration of online and traditional advertising should be present on every kind of advertising you generate. That is, your web address should be in a prominent position on printed matter, e-mails, and signage. Customers do not look at your online business as a separate business. The term *seamless integration* means that businesses are intertwined and one.

What it means is that there are many online advertising opportunities that we are about to reveal in this chapter—but don't throw the baby out with the bathwater. Traditional advertising still works in the right place and when it doesn't cost any extra to do, in the case of signage, existing ads, business cards, and e-mails it is foolish not to do it. If you pass this opportunity it is an opportunity lost.

ONLINE ADVERTISING

Online advertising is a two-edged sword. If done well, it can be terribly effective, generating tons of traffic to and revenue from your web site. On the other hand, done poorly, with slow-loading graphics, annoying popups, or inappropriate placement, online advertising can actually cost you customers!

Here's what you need to know to do things right. There are numerous approaches to online advertising, from the ubiquitous banner ad to the sophisticated web-based tools used by the web's top performers.

BANNER ADS

Banner ads are the Toyota Corolla of the online advertising world. They're everywhere. They're cheap. They work consistently and well. From tiny static buttons sequestered on the bottom corner of a webpage to fully animated minimovies, complete with animation and sound, which stretch across the top of one's screen, banner ads come in a dizzying array of sizes, styles, and formats. Additionally, some banner ads are far more effective than others. We'll tell you why.

What Are Banner Ads

If you put a poodle in a prom dress, what do you get? Well, unless you're really desperate for a date, you've still got a dog. The pretty outfit might get your attention, cause you to look a little closer, but at the end of the day, you're facing a barking, tail-wagging, stick-fetching, bone-gnawing dog.

Banner ads work basically the same way. You've got your poodle—that's the hyperlink sending viewers to your web site once they click on the ad—and you've got the prom dress you've stuffed it into.

In essence, banner ads are nothing more than links—plain old lines of HTML code, strategically placed onto someone else's web site. But no one's going to just click on your link for the heck of it. You've got to entice them. You've got to encourage them. You've got to make them want to see more.

Enter the graphic designers. From fancy fonts and eye catching logos to catchy songs, interactive games, and attractive animated figures, all the bells and whistles have been brought out to dress up the link. Consider it the poodle's prom dress. It's all in place to make people want to look at the dog.

Why Would You Want to Use Banner Ads?

Banner ads serve two purposes. First and foremost, they raise your visibility, creating awareness of your business, and helping create your brand. Second, they drive traffic to your web site.

The first consideration is much more important. Far more people see your banners than will ever click on them. For this reason, it is important that your banner ads reflect your image, consistently mirroring the brand you want the general public to connect with your name. Placing your banners on sites likely to be of interest to your customers—such as a health food company's or an exercise equipment company's site—puts your company's name and logo before the eyes of potential customers, sometimes several times a day. That kind of constant reiteration of your marketing message influences purchasing decisions, even if the viewer doesn't click on the banner.

Banner ads also have the potential to drive traffic to your web site. When viewers click on the ad, they are brought to your web site. This is measured by your click-through rate. You'll see a lot of chatter on the web about declining click-through rates; but the truth is that click-through rates were never spectacularly high. A good click-through rate is between 1 to 2 percent. Does that sound familiar? It's comparable to the response rate to a typical direct mail solicitation, and it costs monumentally less to achieve. Still, in order to maximize potential click-through response, it is vitally important to place your banner ads on web sites that will attract large numbers of your target audience.

Creating

Banner ads can be as simple or as complex as you'd like them to be. The bare-bones model features an image—usually a JPEG or GIF image file—along with some text. From there, you can add as many bells and whistles as you'd like. An animated banner ad displays several images in succession and can be used to create a motion effect. Now, as high-speed Internet becomes more available, the trend is toward rich media banner ads. These ads feature video or audio clips, offer higher levels of interactivity, and incorporate higher-level programming, such as Java or Flash.

Can you do this yourself? Sure—if you're tech-savvy, artistically inclined, and have a good insight into what does and does not constitute an effective ad. Sites exist to help people create banner ads. Some of these sites are:

- *MakeYourBanner.com*
- *ABCBanners.com*

Prefer to outsource? Finding someone to make banners is not difficult. Most graphic or web designers can whip one up for you without any trouble. Prices can start as low as $25 and range quickly upward. We've found a great source of graphic designers to be the advertising departments of local newspapers, especially community shoppers. Most of these folks will happily freelance and are priced very reasonably. However, if you're looking for complex banner ads with lots of high-tech bells and whistles, you're better off going to an established web designer.

Placing

Where your banner appears is as important as what it says. Obviously, you could contact the owners of every web site that you think would be of interest to your target audience, and individually negotiate banner placement rates with them. Some sites will allow you to place banners for free, while others charge based on what is known as the CPM model. With CPM, you pay a set amount—which can range from $5 to well over $100 per thousand clicks. You control where your banners are, and you control how much you're willing to spend on banner advertising. Overall, this works just fine, but be advised it can be extremely time consuming. We can't say for certain, but chances are you might have a few other things on your plate—like running a business, seeing your family, and occasionally sleeping.

Here are some other options:

1. *Banner Exchange Programs*. Trade banners with other advertisers. You agree to post another advertiser's banner on your web site, and he or she displays yours. This is low cost—often free—but you have minimal control over where your banners wind up, and what banners are sent to you to display. However, many banner exchange programs make substantial efforts to keep banners consistent with and appropriate to your web site.

   Some Examples of Banner Exchange Programs:

   • LinkExchange
   • BannerSwap
   • FreeBanners

2. *Banner Ad Networks*. Banner ad networks connect those who want to buy advertising space with those that want to sell it. Consider them the middlemen of the banner advertising world. For a fairly reasonable price, you can have your banner placed on a number of loosely targeted sites. Be aware that much of the market for many banner ad networks comes from large sites, which may not be appropriate if you run a niche-style business. Do your research before making a commitment. That being said,

banner ad networks are a very cost effective way of getting your banner quickly and widely distributed.

POPUP AND INTERSTITIAL ADS

When banner ads became commonplace, some advertisers started looking for new ways to get the user's attention. The reasoning was that users had become numb to banners and could easily ignore them. Rather than relegating themselves to static banner positions, these advertisers turned to popup ads. When the inevitable backlash started against these seemingly random ads that open when a user visits a new webpage, dominating the screen until the user manually closes them, interstitial ads started to appear. These ads also open spontaneously, but close themselves after a few brief seconds.

Both popups and interstitial ads have their advocates, but we're not among them. A good rule of thumb: If web providers are developing tools to block your new advertising technology— and consumers are embracing those tools—the new technology is not a good idea.

GOOGLE ADSENSE

Let's take a minute to look at the other side of the coin. Online advertising isn't all about spending money. There are opportunities to make money as well. One of these is Google AdSense. Google is one of the most trusted names on the net. After all, this company has added itself to the list of those that have become verbs such as Xerox and FedEx. It has capitalized on that trust by creating an innovative ad generation and delivery system.

We've already told you about Google AdWords. In order for Google to offer this service, it also must have a way to place and distribute online advertising. Hence, the Google AdSense program.

Google AdSense works in two ways. You can opt for Google Adsense for Content or Google AdSense Search. Of course, you can implement both methodologies on your site, maximizing the profit stemming from online advertising.

Google AdSense Content consists of small, unobtrusive ads provided by Google that you place on content-laden pages of your site. These ads will be relevant to your content—for example, your article, "How to Install a Tub Surround," might receive ads for shower mats, waterproof adhesive, or rubber ducks—without competing with your products. You can either use pay per click compensation or pay by impression (related to how often the ad appears on your site). Obviously, the more traffic your site receives and the more clicks the ad gets the more lucrative this proposition becomes.

Google AdSense Search entails adding a Google search box to your web site. Visitors use the search feature, which then delivers search result pages—complete with targeted ads. When a visitor clicks on an ad, you get paid.

To qualify for Google AdSense, your site must meet certain criteria. These include:

- Your site must be working—no dead links!
- Your site must be easily navigable.
- Your site must contain content—no advertising-only sites!
- Your site cannot contain any prohibited items. This includes hate speech and sale of prohibited items, including weapons, drugs, alcohol, and tobacco, among other things.

SUPER PAGES

Super Pages is the next generation of the phonebook—all grown up and getting comfortable in cyberspace. While the traditional paper phone book is still going strong, Verizon and Super Pages have developed a web-based directory, accessible and relevant to the entire country. In addition to business profile pages, this searchable computerized directory offers webpage, phone, and physical address listings to users.

Add-ons include preferred placement, sponsored links, banner ad placement, and the ability to access Super Pages' Spanish-language version.

A great deal of Super Pages' appeal is its strong resemblance to traditional phone books. This makes it very relevant and easily accessible to many older Internet users, who grew using a phone book. Currently, this demographic consists of users of both genders, 35 and older, who are responsible for the majority of major purchases made online. If your business is particularly targeting this demographic, a listing in SuperPages may be a wise idea. As the population grows older and the purchasing power shifts to younger generation, Super Pages may need to change formats in order to remain relevant. The focus on business profile pages, sponsored links, and banner placement are the earliest signs of this transition.

DOUBLECLICK

DoubleClick is very different than the other sites discussed in this section. Rather than creating advertising or selling advertising space, DoubleClick concentrates on the planning and management of online advertising campaigns. While this may seem beyond the pale for many small business owners, utilizing a sophisticated set of analysis and management tools related to web advertising may be of interest as online operations become more central to your business model.

DoubleClick's DART system—which stands for Dynamic Advertising Reporting and Targeting—analyzes users who visit a webpage enabled with DART technology. Multiple criteria are assessed, from time of day and number of times the site was accessed to more individualized data, such as the user's physical location. These data are used to deliver specifically selected advertisements in an effort to meet the advertiser's needs and capture the user's interest. Obviously, using DoubleClick's services requires a serious commitment to online advertising, as well as a depth of web ads to appeal to a variety of users.

Chapter 14's Essential Essentials

1. Don't ignore traditional forms of advertising.
2. Make sure your web address appears in all your advertising and signage and e-mails.
3. Consider banner ad as part of your marketing.
4. Explore banner ad exchange programs.
5. Popup ads might work but simply not with the backlash you'll get.
6. Investigate the use of AdSense as buyer and seller and see if it makes sense for your business.
7. Service businesses and any business that does well with Yellow Pages should strongly consider listing with Super Pages.
8. Consider using DoubleClick when you become serious about online advertising. It's the difference between knowing and not knowing what works. It takes the guess work out of addressing.

For more information on this topic, go to

www.essentialonlinesolution.com.

Chapter 15

Viral Marketing

Do you know who is pregnant?
Did you hear who is having an affair?
I know something you'd love to know!
It's a secret!
Promise not to tell anyone?
What a great service and it's free!
They have the best . . .
You gotta go to . . .

Those words and phrases are the essence of viral marketing. It's all about news we just love to spread. Rumors, chain letters with warnings, gossip, secondhand accounts, or even leaked information are at the core of viral marketing. Maybe there is a little bit of the town crier in all of us.

The twist is manipulating the buzz into profitability. We have to come clean—we hate the term *viral marketing*. But isn't the term viral marketing a true testament to viral marketing?

Huh?

What does that mean?

The term *viral marketing* was popularized and has become part of our vocabulary. But it's not really the most accurate description of what it is. Viral marketing is an urban myth. How did viral marketing ever get adopted as a form of marketing? A virus is not a nice thing. Viruses can kill. Viruses screw up computers. Just because something spreads quickly we call it a virus. Researchers, doctors, scientists, work to stop viruses.

WORD-OF-MOUTH ADVERTISING

This isn't something new that was created in the 1990s. This has been going on for centuries. Years ago we didn't call it *plague marketing*. We called it one thing and that is word-of-mouth advertising or what we call *WOMA*. Some call it creating the buzz.

But who is kidding who—it's WOMA. Ask any business person the best form of advertising and he or she will tell you it's word-of-mouth. WOMA. Actually, a recent SBA study indicated that 87 percent of small business customers will come from referrals or word-of-mouth.

This is a chapter that combines many traditional values of marketing, some interesting concepts, a dose of common sense mixed together with some high-tech spice to create a killer way to promote a business.

What's changed? Nothing and everything. Let's first address the *Everything*. *Everything* can actually be summed up in a word: Speed. Information can travel so much faster today because of the web and e-mail. Just a few short years ago word traveled as fast as we could dial a number and spread because of the multiples of one person telling 10 people who told 10 people and on and on. But that took time. Now anyone can send an e-mail to their entire address book in less than a minute. Then all of those people can do the same and on and on. Then add in the fact that distance doesn't matter and there is *no* cost other than time and you realize how everything has changed.

So why did we say that nothing has changed? We believe that because the basic principles have not changed. We talk about the *wows* in life and business. Isn't it strange that the word *wow* is 50 percent of WOMA? We talk about the different, the unusual, the things that are newsworthy, out of the ordinary, and things that exceed our expectations.

There is one basic disconnect in business today. Everyone understands the importance of word-of-mouth advertising; but what they fail to appreciate is if you want WOMA, then you must give people something to talk about. *"Give 'em Something to Talk about"* or what we call *GESTA*. The expression we live by is:

THERE IS NO WOMA WITHOUT GESTA.

Having good service, selection of goods or services, and good prices are in themselves nothing to talk about. If you don't have good service, a good selection or products or services, or fair and competitive prices, you're not even in business today. That is what is expected today. It is about the service that's out of the ordinary, the kind of service that built Nordstrom's. It's about the selection that Amazon has with books, which is basically any book ever written. They make a superstore look like a convenience store in comparison. As for price, it is what has launched more viral/ WOMA campaigns then anything else. But it wasn't just a low price that won the web, it was *free* that was the tipping point.

The classic example that pundits love to refer to as the best example of viral marketing is *Hotmail.com*. It was the first free form of web-based e-mail services. The strategy is simple:

1. Give away free e-mail addresses and services.
2. Attach a tag at the bottom of every free message sent out: "Get your private, free e-mail at *http://www.hotmail.com.*"
3. Then stand back while people e-mail to their own network of friends and associates.

The *wow* that created the WOMA was free. Google became the superstar that it is because of a few factors. It was just better than everybody else and it was free. Then it became committed to find other services to offer for free such as maps, directions, e-mail services, picture organization, and even a helpful toolbar that of course makes it easier to use Google.

Each time Google added a service it gained a new platform for its pinpointed advertising program that was not only cost-effective advertising, fairly priced (the marketplace determines the price via bidding), but it figured out how to make money so that it can invest in other ways to offer free and fee services. What a concept!

B. Good: A Good Example of WOMA

We are involved in the Retailers Association of Massachusetts. In 1997, Rick started an awards program called the *RAMAES*, the Retailers Association of Massachusetts Awards of Excellence. The association gave its 2005 award for Restaurant of the Year to a healthy fast-food store that had only been in business for 18 months. The name of the business is B. Good. The name came from an expression that an eccentric uncle would say to two best friends every time they would leave, be good. That has relevance because the eccentric Uncle Ferris became the core part of a very sophisticated viral marketing business launch from these two friends. The business sells good food fast and everything it does is designed to get people talking about it.

The owners believe in WOMA marketing in every aspect of their marketing. First in their signs such as: "We like turkey so much that we gently grind it, hand pack it into beautiful patties, and serve it with a big stupid smile." Another sign that captures your imagination is: "Just yesterday, our veggie burgers were spinach, portabellas, red peppers, and beans. Veggie burgers grow up so fast nowadays." And yet another sign says: "Our French fries are precious, baked slices of love from potato heaven. We never cook them in recycled boiling grease. That just wouldn't be right."

When was one of the last time you talked about the signs at McDonald's?

B. Good also has an interesting approach to signing people up to its electronic newsletter. The sign in the store says: "Join our family. Get our newsletter. Read our stories, watch stupid videos, enter weird contests, and eat delicious burgers for free. Join our family at *www.bgood.com*."

This company has spent less than $1,000 on advertising and PR yet has a mailing list of over 10,000 people. Pretty good, wouldn't you say? Not to mention it has a minimum of 30 major news stories written about it. Another one of B. Good's tactics is that anyone who receives its newsletter gets free food. It might be a new sandwich B. Good is featuring or a classic sandwich. As the two 30-something owners say, "We'd rather pay our customers for advertising than the newspapers."

It gets even better.

The owners also believe in having off-the-wall contests to get people talking. They have created a Hall of Fame of Cousins. In order to make it to the Hall of Fame, you have to win one of the contests that are generally about naming a product.

One of the contests became famous: Customer of the Year. But the spin B. Good put on Customer of the Year is that the customer receives free food for the year. How does it choose the winner?

People have to write something to be a contender. So, you have contestants writing a short essay about why they want to be customer of the year and you get a whole bunch of copy and compliments about your business. Who wouldn't talk about that to their friends?

B. Good also purchased an 18-year-old El Camino car that it had painted with flames running up the side. The restaurant then had a contest to name the El Camino. The winning name was "El Tio," and the owners now park the car in front of the restaurant. But one of the more interesting contests at B. Good is called the "Garlicky Green" contest. Again people have to write in telling why they deserve to become a finalist/contender to compete in the finals in the store. The finals consist of people eating bowls of spinach with garlic on it. Again the winner gets free food for a year.

The owners' business philosophy is to market to the 1 percent of your market base that will get involved in these crazy competitions. Those are the ones who will create word-of-mouth advertising for you. It is their philosophy, but it happens to work pretty well.

Making WOMA Work for You

So how can you create a WOMA marketing campaign for your business?

WOMA marketing depends on a high pass-along rate from person to person. How do you do it if you are a plumber, insurance agent, or an accountant?

Let's start with the plumber. In every presentation that Rick does, he talks about the use of fun, humor, and playful behavior that creates wonderful WOMA marketing—and he shows a slide of a plumber that creates more WOMA marketing than any other visual example we can think of. A plumber has painted on the door of the driver's side of his van a man sitting on a toilet. The man lacks a head, but that is supplied by the plumber driving the john, er, van. You never forget the plumber. It's an example of humor that generates word-of-mouth advertising.

Humor is a great pass along tool. For proof, look at how many people forward e-mail jokes to you. That's why, in a previous section of the book when we talked about e-mail marketing, we suggested putting a joke in each of your e-mails.

Another example of visual word-of-mouth advertising is from a paint and wallpaper store. It had a sign that read: "Husbands selecting paint must have a note from wife." Everyone talks about that and spreads it around.

CLEND

What we have just discussed is traditional word-of-mouth advertising. How do you bridge that into a *clend*—click and send?

Clend is another one of our key phrases. The goal is to send something so good that you create a *clend:* something that is clicked on and sent forward. As good as a *clend* is the goal is to create a multiple *clend*, which means you are forwarding the e-mail to multiple people. As we stated in an earlier chapter, one of Rick's newsletter recipients *clend* 187 times a week. Now that's the beauty of WOMA.

What we are talking about is creating intentional WOMA. You want to control the process by getting your message into the places and into the hands of those who will *clend* it the most.

WOMA MARKETING STEPS

So what are the steps to WOMA marketing?

Step One: Killer Content

Do you have something that is so revolutionary that it generates the clend you desire? What are the categories of killer content? This is not copy that we are talking about here. We are talking about the offer, the news, or the motivator that will make people click. Here are some examples:

- Faster
- Cheaper
- Sexier
- Greed
- Love
- Hunger
- Being popular
- Fear
- Revolutionary
- Status
- Fun and humor
- Last and most important, personal health or vanity

An interesting example is a friend of ours, Steve Shapiro, who wrote a great book, *Goal-Free Living*. It is endorsed by some very prestigious writers and professionals. Now, with a title like that and the endorsements, you would think that would be enough to create strong word-of-mouth advertising and produce the necessary *clend* that he would need to make it a best seller.

However, he chose a way to accelerate the process by making the killer content a deal you could not refuse. He sent out a well-organized offering to anyone who was willing to purchase his book on a certain day in order to obtain a high ranking on Amazon and *barnesandnoble.com*. In the e-mail he offered $1,000 worth of free stuff, mostly in the form of publication or special reports, for all those people who purchased the book and special incentives for anyone who bought multiple copies. It was an extremely successful campaign. We used this example because it demonstrates the different elements of a WOMA campaign.

Step Two: Create Alliances or Affinity Programs

Create alliances or build affinity programs with other businesses selling to the same marketplace. What we mean by this is asking other people to send out your notice to their mailing list. A women's clothing store might be catering to the same group of people who buy jewelry. A plumber can market to the same list of people that electricians or painters use. When a person refers a business that he is pleased with, that referral becomes the strongest referral you can get.

Step Three: Endorsements

Michael Jordan endorsed Nike sneakers and the product took off. That cost Nike millions. You can get industry endorsements and customer endorsements. Get as many endorsements as possible from your best-known customers, not necessarily your best customers. Look for the local celebrity who wants the exposure more than he or she wants money. The more prestigious the person in your field, industry, or in the general public, the more powerful the referral and the more people will talk about it.

Step Four: Topics of Interest

When offering some type of bonus or incentive to entice people to buy now, look for incentives that are a *wow* or information that caters to the market you are appealing to. Once in Rick's women's retail store, he offered an incentive for a free motor scooter for the winner of a store contest. There was only one problem: No one wanted it. Instead of giving the motor scooter, the store kept giving store gift certificates to the winners who didn't want the bike. Make sure it's something they want. Also, look for information you can package together that can be used as an incentive.

Step Five: Personalize

Personalize your e-mails as much as possible by using the recipient's name in the heading and in the body of the text. It just softens up your approach.

Step Six: Test

Test different headlines, subject lines, styles, and even products until you finally reach the right items or mix of items. Test whenever possible. Ask your friends, colleagues, and family for specific and honest feedback. But don't get caught up with "paralysis by analysis."

Step Seven: Use the Autoblaster Concept

Steve Waterhouse, author and consultant from Jacksonville, Florida, created the *autoblaster* concept, which is a line in the next to last paragraph of every article that he writes that says, "If you would like further information (a white paper or special report) about the topic, click here." It will open up to an e-mail page where all of your contact information is on the bottom and you'll be collecting a list of people who are interested in your topic.

Step Eight: Track and Analyze Results

How many of your e-mails are opened, how many are passed along, and how many are clicked through? And what percentage of those that have clicked through actually took action? These numbers are vital to planning your marketing strategy. Be sure to track them, but even more important, use them!

TWO KEY THOUGHTS

What you are offering is a sample of what you do. You're letting someone use, try, or have a portion of what you do for free. We are working on the premise that the more people who are exposed to the idea or product, the more people will use it. Similar to sampling is the use of statistics, polls, and surveys— anything for which someone would like to see the results.

You are trying to make an emotional connection when you do WOMA marketing. Logic makes us think and shop but emotions make us buy. Make sure you have that emotional tug with every campaign you do.

Chapter 15's Essential Essentials

1. Be clear on the WOMA (word of mouth advertising) market base.
2. Use GESTA (give 'em something to talk about) to define what you will give them.
3. Estimate your pass-along rate.
4. Follow the WOMA marketing steps as outlined.
5. Give a sampling of your work.
6. Touch the emotions of your audience.

For more information on this topic, go to

www.essentialonlinesolution.com.

Step V

Sell, Sell, Sell

Chapter 16

Going, Going, Gone—
eBay and Online Auctions

Are They Right for You?

Imagine a sales force that never sleeps. A store that never closes. A shop that is conveniently located—for all of your customers! That's the attraction of online auctions—constant availability, and easy access for all.

Add to that attraction that online auctions are extremely popular. eBay, far and away the largest online auction, reports that in the first six months of 2005, members sold 10.6 billion dollars worth of merchandise. One-third of all the people who use the Internet in the United States have visited eBay at least once. That's approximately 35 million individuals, which is an awful lot of potential customers.

eBay is not the only game in town. We'll be referencing eBay throughout this chapter because it is the industry leader. But we'll also mention other players. There are dozens of online auction sites, some serving specific, narrow niches, while others are wide open. As more Americans become comfortable shopping online—and a staggering 42 percent were already buying goods and services over the net in 2004!—traffic at all of these auction sites will only increase.

Best of all, selling via online auction is easy. Really easy. People who don't have any formal education, much less advanced degrees or business experience, have gone on to make fortunes on eBay. A joint study done by eBay and the U.S. Post Office in 2005 indicated that nearly three-quarters of a million people— 724,000 to be exact—rely upon eBay sales as a source of primary or secondary income.

What does this mean for your small business? Are there ways that your company can incorporate online auctions into your existing sales efforts? Can you afford not to? Read on, and we'll tell you.

ARE ONLINE AUCTIONS RIGHT FOR MY SMALL BUSINESS?

Online auctions are a very versatile sales tool. You can do all your sales via online auction, or you can view auctions to augment to your existing operation. By adding online auctions to your current sales strategies, you're vastly increasing the number of potential customers you reach every single day. You're also creating the opportunity to create new customer sales incentives, and gain access to a new promotional tool. Best of all, participating in online auctions can actually drive traffic to your existing web site, generating additional sales!

The Internet is a great equalizer. It's a given that small businesses value their customers more and go out of their way to provide better service—the trick is initially finding those customers. With online auctions, the smallest mom-and-pop shop located in the exact center of nowhere can reach customers far beyond the range of their traditional marketing efforts. This allows the small business owner to offer consumers an alternative to the mega-corporations—and access to the trademark customer service and individual attention that makes small businesses unique.

Yet larger companies do have some advantages. Deeper pockets allow them to finance market research, to conduct promotional campaigns, and to engage in far more advertising than the average small business owner. Small businesses often don't have the budget to engage in these activities, especially when there's an element of risk involved. After all, if Wal-Mart spends $50,000 on a particular advertising campaign, that's merely a drop in a behemoth marketing budget. But ask a small business owner to sink $50,000 into advertising, and ... well, we can hear you laughing from here.

Online auctions level this particular corner of the playing field. By providing small business owners with three distinct benefits that they may not otherwise have access to, online auctions open the door for small business to expand their operation at minimal cost. These three benefits are expanded markets, creating new consumer incentives, and access to a free promotional tool, generating traffic to your independent web site. We'll discuss each individually.

Expanded Markets

The first, and greatest, advantage of online auctions is immediate access to greatly expanded markets. You already know how many customers you get with no Internet presence at all. Poorly designed and utilized web sites don't yield much better results—after all, that's why you've bought this book! Using the other tools and strategies you'll find here, you can increase traffic and sales generated from your web site.

Yet no matter how you improve your own personal web site, you'll never create a site with the drawing power of eBay. By working with an established marketplace, you're tapping into a huge pool of existing customers—customers who otherwise may have never even known that your product existed, much less searched for your web site.

The potential scope of the marketplace is staggering. Above and beyond the millions of shoppers who regularly visit eBay and other online auction sites in the United States, consider the growing community of people who use eBay all around the world. There are auction sites for Australia, Austria, Belgium, Canada, China, France, Germany, Hong Kong, India, Ireland, Italy, Malaysia, the Netherlands, New Zealand, Poland, the Philippines, Singapore, South Korea, Spain, Sweden, Switzerland, Taiwan, and the United Kingdom, giving you access to countries you may never have considered selling to!

Creating New Customer Sales Incentives

Consider the golf club. Despite what Tiger Woods might argue, golf clubs are not traditionally considered a necessity. They're expensive. They last a long time. How often are you going to buy a golf club?

The answer: Probably not very often. In fact, in Scotland, where the game was born, some modern day duffers pride themselves on playing with the same clubs their grandfathers carried onto the links many years before.

Yet new golf club models come out every year. How can the average golfer—perhaps less sentimental than our Scottish example, but still with one eye on his wallet—justify purchasing new clubs when his or her current clubs are still perfectly good?

Enter the trade-in. By offering to buy back last year's clubs when a player purchases new ones, our retailer has created an incentive program that enables his customer to continually trade up. In fact, for some players, this very scenario has become a yearly tradition.

Yet what are retailers going to do with all the old clubs? They're still relatively new, still in good condition—many haven't been used more than a dozen times! Enter the online auction.

According to Andy Schechter, owner of *GolfClubExchange.com*, this model allows small retailers to engage in trade-in programs on a far greater scale than ever before. *Excess inventory can be moved via online auction,* whether at a specialist auction site like his or at an all-purpose auction site like eBay. Shoppers happily snap up the latest models, especially at auction prices—while sellers not only recoup their trade-in expense but earn a secondary profit!

This model can work with any number of products, but works especially well with those items with a high initial cost, that remain in good condition, retain their value, and that consumers are prone to upgrading frequently. Do your products qualify? Trade-in potential may exist—and a specialty auction site may already be in place to accommodate your needs. Schechter runs a similar auction site for musical instruments and is about to open one for fine jewelry.

AUCTIONS AS A PROMOTIONAL TOOL

Perhaps one of the most powerful aspects of online auctions is also one of the most commonly overlooked. Done properly, online auctions have the potential to generate additional sales for your small business above and beyond the initial sale. Online auctions are also a great way to introduce a new product and generate buzz among your target audience.

Key to making the most of the promotional aspects of participating in online auctions is fully understanding the many features each auction site offers. It's imperative to carefully read the rules of each auction site. For example, eBay does not allow outbound links in their listings—but it does offer an *About Me* page where sellers can describe their business and link directly to their web site. Remarkably few sellers take advantage of this feature.

Careful listing writing is essential. Savvy sellers write the copy of their listings to include their business name. To comply with most auction site rules, this must be done in a way that cannot be construed as advertising, such as:

- There is more information about this widget on *BlueWidget. com*, where you'll also find interesting articles and a user guide.
- They'll also find descriptions of your products and services, of course, but don't mention that in this listing, or you'll be violating auction site regulations.

Another promotional strategy is to use online auctions to sell informational products, such as an e-book, at a minimal price— say one penny. People purchase the e-book, and are e-mailed a link to your download page. Make sure your download page encourages visitors to explore what's on the rest of the site. Send them to a fairly blank page with no splash, and you've wasted your time.

Online auctions are also a good way to generate buzz around a new product. Strategically placing listings in categories visited by your target audience will raise awareness of the new product, generate sales, and help drive demand. It may also result in some unexpected profit. The special dynamic of the auction atmosphere has often resulted in many buyers paying two to three times retail price for a new product—even though they could easily purchase the exact same product and pay half the price by visiting the seller's web site!

WHAT ARE ONLINE AUCTIONS?

What, exactly, is eBay? You may think you know, but if you ask a dozen people, you'll get a dozen answers. Some will tell you that eBay is the place to find great products at rock bottom prices. Others will let you know that eBay is a collector's dream, offering up rare one-of-a-kind items worth hundreds, even thousands of dollars. Still more will tell you that eBay is an *efficient product delivery system*, allowing business owners to discover new markets and find customers for their products all over the world. And finally, some see eBay as an end in itself, setting up businesses specifically to sell via online auctions. Apparently, eBay has managed the impossible. It's become all things to all people.

That can't be right, can it? After all, we're told you can't please all of the people all of the time.

Yet eBay manages to come pretty darn close. Bargain shoppers and fine art collectors browse the same web site, use the same search tools, and pay for their purchases the same way. Sure, one may be looking for baby clothes while the next searches for Cartier watches, but the underlying mechanism is the same.

Reduced to its simplest essence, eBay and other online auctions work by providing a virtual location where individual buyers and sellers can connect. Sellers upload listings, which generally include a brief description and photograph of the item in question, set some price parameters, and determine how long they want the auction to run. Buyers browse among the thousands of listings, find items of interest, place bids indicating how much they're willing to pay, and if they are the winning bidder, purchase the item.

There are countless bells and whistles that have been added onto this basic framework. Sellers can pay for prominent placement of their listings, list individual items in multiple categories to increase the likelihood of sales, and even create *Storefronts* or *Online Stores*, under the umbrella of the auction site.

Learning how to access all the features of any given online auction site may seem intimidating, but online auction sites go out of their way to teach sellers how to use the site easily. eBay even offers eBay Universities, with both online and in-the-class-room settings, to teach aspiring sellers how to do a good job.

WHAT DIFFERENT ONLINE AUCTIONS SERVICES ARE THERE?

eBay is far and away the largest online auction service. It offers a full range of products, from junk mail to diamond rings, and everything in between.

Some subsequent auction sites followed the eBay model, providing a platform for buyers and sellers to trade in an almost endless variety of products. Others opted for the specialist route, limiting transactions to a specific type of product, such as books, musical instruments, or cars.

Table 16.1 shows a dozen examples of each type of online auction site. This list is by no means exhaustive—new auction sites appear daily, sometimes even hourly!

Why the Difference?

If you find yourself pondering why there are two types of online auction sites, take a look at the medical world. Some physicians are general practitioners, dealing with every patient who walks through the door, and treating a wide variety of problems. Other physicians are specialists—cardiologists, gastroenterologists,

Table 16.1   Auction Sites

All-Purpose Auction Sites	Specialist Auction Sites
Yahoo Auctions	GolfClubExchange.com
Amazon.com	InstrumentExchange.com
Ubid.com	Bid4Vacations.com
Ebid.com	Potteryauction.com
Overstock.com	MothersNature.com
Bidz.com	JustBeads.com

even podiatrists—and address a very narrow range of specific problems.

To carry the analogy further, someone who has a problem—a fractured big toe—may go to the general practitioner, knowing that there's a fairly good chance that he may be able to get his toe fixed there. Or he may opt to head to the podiatrist, where there's a much higher probability that someone well trained in medical issues pertaining to the foot could address his busted big toe.

Auctions work the same way. If Barbara is looking for a stained glass lamp for her front hall, she may opt to go to an all-purpose auction site. After all, lots of people are selling lots of things, and chances are that somewhere among the throngs of sellers, there's someone looking to unload a stained glass lamp.

But what if Barbara really wants that stained glass lamp? She might opt to go to a specialty stained glass auction site, where all she'll find is stained glass items. Chances are that there will be a wider variety of lamps available, with higher quality and specialty items to choose from.

What do you do if you're a smart small business owner? You research what specialty auction sites pertain to your industry. List your items there—*and* on the all-purpose auction sites. That way your products are in front of the widest possible audience.

THE NUTS AND BOLTS OF ONLINE AUCTIONS

So now we've convinced you. This online auction thing sounds like a good idea, and you want a piece of the action for yourself. The only problem is, you don't know how to get started.

Luckily, online auction sites are very user friendly. eBay even has a Live Help button on every page. Click on this when you get stuck, and an eBay staffer will be chatting with you within seconds. This is an incredibly helpful feature.

Rather than try to reinvent the wheel here, we're going to direct you to the experts rather than try to teach you how to use the most popular online auction sites. Listed in Table 16.2, you'll find links to tutorial pages for each of these sites. There you'll find complete instructions, walking you through the entire process. These sites are constantly changing and evolving, as the online auction world is a very dynamic place. There was no need to have rules in place prohibiting the sale of human organs, for example, until someone tried to do exactly that.

If we've just completely ruined your great shiny new business idea with that last sentence, we're very, very sorry—and more than a little scared.

Table 16.2   Auction Tutorials

Links To Online Auction Tutorials

eBay—*http://pages.eBay.com/education/*
Yahoo Auctions—*http://help.yahoo.com/help/us/auct/asell/*
Ubid.com—*http://www.ubid.com/help/topic1.asp*
Overstock.com—*http://auctions.overstock.com/*
  (Click on the Auctions tab, then click on Help and access the FAQ section.)

Equipment Needed

To participate in online auctions, you'll need some equipment. You'll be glad to know that this is one instance where gearing up is easy. Most of this equipment is very common and has multiple applications. Chances are you own this stuff already. In addition to the items you intend to sell, you need:

- *Computer system with Internet access*. High speed is better, especially when uploading pictures of your stock, but plenty of people run successful auction businesses on dial-up.
- *Digital camera or scanner*. To create and upload pictures of your items. Items without pictures don't sell. This is one instance where the "a picture is worth a thousand words" truism is very, very accurate.

And that's it! We told you this was easy.

THE TWO POINTS TO MAKING MONEY

We're going to tell you a little secret here, something that we've learned through decades of retail experience and in-depth research. Online auction success depends primarily on two factors: *What You Sell* and *How You Sell It*. If you think that doesn't sound any different than regular off-the-web business, you're right. And you're wrong.

Online auction customers have been socialized to have certain expectations. They know what they want to see from a web site, from an auction listing, and from a seller. These expectations are completely different than the expectations these customers have when they walk into a brick-and-mortar store.

Online auction customers have more questions. They can't physically see the items they're considering, can't pick them up, feel the quality, assess the value. All they have to depend upon is you—and they're going to put you to the test. Even if you think you know everything there is to know about your product, someone is going to come up with a question you never, ever expected.

On the other hand, the same customer service skills you've honed in the development of your small business are crucial here. Online auctions are rife with rude, unprofessional, even offensive sellers. Customers would prefer to deal with someone pleasant and customer orientated. If that becomes your reputation, you'll win hordes of loyal buyers.

What You Sell

We're going to split this section into two parts. Part one is for those of you who are going to use online auctions as another sales channel for your existing business. It discusses choosing products from your existing stock, how many products to sell online, and some subtle factors that go into determining what does and does not make a good auction item. Part two is for those of you who have read this far thinking, "Hmmm...maybe I could start a whole new business, with online auctions as my point of entry!" Don't be shy. We started thinking that way ourselves...and we're the ones who wrote the book!

Part One

When considering using online auctions as an additional sales channel for your business, you must first determine what role you want auctions to play. Are you using auctions primarily as a sales generating tool, or is your focus more promotional, with an eye toward driving buyers toward your existing web site? This will determine what percentage of your stock should be sold via online auctions.

If you are planning on making the majority of your online sales through an auction site, you will want to have a larger percentage of your inventory listed. However, if you are using auctions as a promotional tool, it is better to limit the number of items available via auction and use the desire for more items to drive buyers to your individual web site. This is an individual decision, based largely on what type of items you sell, the range of price points you have (many sellers prefer not to put extremely high-end items up for auction), and the physical size of the items involved. Additionally, if you do custom or individual work for your clients as well as your standard product line, you may not wish to auction those services, to avoid getting locked into an unprofitable situation.

Part Two

If you are planning to start a whole new business with online auctions as your entry point, you've got a certain advantage. You can make your product decisions based on what sells, rather than being tied to an inventory that you are emotionally or financially invested in.

The most popular categories on eBay, and subsequently, where most sales are made, include:

- Collectibles
- eBay Motors (automobiles)
- Computers
- Electronics
- Clothes
- Shoes
- Toys

Most successful online auction sellers find a niche, specializing in one or two types of items. Before you settle on a niche, ask yourself the following questions:

- Do I have an interest in this type of item?
- Do I have any particular expertise that will make selling this item easier?
- Can I store my inventory while I'm waiting for it to sell? It is far easier to store shoes than cars!
- Are there seasonal fluctuations in this marketplace? Lawn mowers don't sell well in February.
- Can I turn a good profit on these items?
- Is it difficult to ship? Buyers shy away from heavy items with high shipping costs. Likewise, fragile items that require careful packaging might be a headache for you.

Another option is working with a wholesaler. Increasing numbers of auction sellers act as conduits for wholesalers. *Drop-ship* options mean the seller has nothing to do but arrange the sale and collect the money.

If you're interested in this option, finding a reputable company to work with is key. There are scads of companies on the Internet offering listings of wholesalers for anywhere from $5 to well over $100. Keep your money in your wallet. Instead, approach finding a wholesaler the way you would find any other vendor. Do your research, check references, examine sample products, and make your decisions based on hard numbers.

What to Avoid: There are products, services, and other items that cannot be sold via online auction. Some of these are common sense: Illegal drugs, live animals, explosives. Others may not leap immediately to mind: Seeds, postage meters, and firearms.

How You Sell

Unlike what you sell, how you sell remains constant. Online auctions are driven by listings. Writing a good listing is an art and a science.

Questionable Items

eBay maintains a list of questionable items that may or may not be sold, determination of which is made on a case-by-case basis. Indeed, every auction site has its own regulations. eBay's are here:

- http://pages.eBay.com/help/sell/item_allowed.html

Listings are your opportunity to sell the item. Central to this is a clear description of what you're actually selling. The three points this description must have include:

1. Complete name of the item
2. Accurate physical description, including dimensions if appropriate
3. Comment on condition

All of these features will be supported by your photographs. Use your remaining space to sell the item—using words that will capture the buyer's attention, without misrepresenting the item. Here's where the art of selling comes in. You're writing advertising copy. What would make you want to buy this item? We can't even tell you how many clothing listings we saw during our research that read: "I bought this and put it on and it looked ugly on me. Am cleaning out my closet."

Now, doesn't that make you want to rush out and buy that outfit? People, please! Truth in advertising is one thing, shooting yourself in the foot is another. Be honest, but be enticing, engaging, and different. We once saw a pair of leather pants from the late 1970s sell for several hundred dollars because the seller told a humorous story detailing why he bought the pants, how come he never had the courage to actually wear the pants, what kind of man he hoped to be when he bought the pants, and what kind of man he actually turned out to be.

Another seller, sticking to a dry recitation of the bare essential facts, would have been lucky to get $10 for those pants. Auction shoppers are looking for the story just as much as the product. Creativity garners higher prices.

In your description, certain words will help propel you to the top of numerous search categories. These words, often sought terms, are called keywords. You'll hear a lot of buzz about keywords, but they're really very simple. What are the hot words, the things people search for most on the Internet? This changes every week, sometimes every day, and on eBay it can change by the hour. Yet some points remain consistent. We've spelled those out in our Dos and Don'ts of Keywords in Table 16.3.

Table 16.3   The Do's and Don'ts of Keywords

Do Use as many keywords as you legitimately can. Use brand names, descriptions, and identifying details to grab attention. Model numbers and designer names work well.

Don't Use words like LOOK! or WOW! Nobody searches for WOW!

Do Detail exactly what the item is. It's okay if this repeats the category headings.

Don't Misrepresent using keywords. Saying "Looks like Chanel" or "If you like Grand Theft Auto" to get included in searches for Chanel or Grand Theft Auto will get you bumped off the auction site.

Do Think like your buyer. Include terms your buyer would be likely to search for, for example: Pink Easter Dress Size 6.

Don't Keyword spam. This includes loading your listing with all kinds of keywords that have little, if anything, to do with your product.

Do Pay special attention to listing titles. Most people search by title. Generally, your titles can be up to 55 characters long. Use them all.

eBAY STORES

eBay stores are mini-web sites provided by eBay to give sellers a special place to sell their inventory. Listing an item in an eBay store costs a fraction of what it costs to list an item in a regular auction—about 3 cents per item in an eBay store versus 10 to 15 percent of the selling price of an item in auction!

Reasons to consider eBay stores:

- Benefit from high traffic affiliated with eBay.
- Low cost way to advertise slow moving inventory.
- Increasingly popular as eBay changes listing model: Items in eBay stores are now appearing after traditional auction items appear on a search.

SHIPPING, HANDLING, AND INSURANCE

Your success with eBay and other online auction sites hinges on your ability to ship items quickly and well. The most successful sellers send items out as soon as payment is received, often the same day.

Package items very carefully. Broken items are extremely disappointing—to buyers who don't get their expected item—and to you, who will have to refund their money. The U.S. Postal Service—shipper of choice for most eBay sellers, due to lower rates and wide service area—has an online shipper's guide at *http://www.usps.com/consumers/domestic.htm*.

Insurance is a necessity when shipping high-end or fragile items, and often a wise idea for other items. Most sellers have buyers assume the cost of insurance, or declaim all responsibility for the item once it leaves their possession.

Shipping items internationally can be tricky. The U.S. Postal Service does not offer the tracking services private freight carriers offer, but private freight companies are subject to more stringent customs and paperwork requirements. For this reason, most foreign buyers insist their purchases be shipped via U.S. Postal Service. Do your research and weigh your options before completing international transactions.

DO YOU TAKE PAYPAL: WHAT YOU NEED TO KNOW ABOUT ONLINE PAYMENT SYSTEMS

With the millions of transactions and billions of dollars that have move through eBay, financial safety and security are an issue. While some buyers still prefer to do business by sending a personal check or money order to the seller (who then has to wait for the check to clear!), increasing numbers prefer the speed and convenience of paying with a bank or credit card. Yet in these days of identity theft, you don't want to hand your credit card information over willy-nilly to some person you've never met.

Enter PayPal.

By acting as a middleman, PayPal facilitates online auction sales. Buyers pay the money to PayPal, who then transfers it to the seller's account. Setting up an account is quick and easy. You can find out more here at *http://www.paypal.com.*

THE VALUE OF RESEARCH

One day, when you've got a spare couple of hours, use Google and search *eBay advice*. You'll be astonished at what springs up. There are hundreds, even thousands of books, newsletters, web sites, and seminars all promising to help you make the most of the online auction experience.

Unique among these are the special reports that promise to tell you what to sell, when to sell, and reams of market research to back up the claims. Opinions of this type of data are split in the online auction world. Some very successful sellers swear by the stuff, claiming that knowing that most auctions close on 5 P.M. on Friday allows them to time their sales appropriately. Others, equally successful, claim that they've read the research and found nothing of value. They assert that sound business practices are all any online auction seller needs to be successful.

The truth is probably somewhere in the middle. It doesn't hurt to have some insight into the buying habits of auction buyers—after all, it is kind of interesting to note that most eBay shoppers are 35 or older, make at least $35,000 annually, and are slightly more likely to be male. On the other hand, you still need sound business practices.

Our advice: Find one or two sources that you trust, and get your data from them. There's no reason to purchase every book, newsletter, and special report that comes along. We pay particular attention to insight coming from those with a proven track record and good reputation, as well as courses offered by eBay or other major online auction sites.

Be wary of those gurus who claim you can trick or cheat eBay. Follow their strategies, and you might just wind up with a heap of trouble.

TOP POINTS FROM AUCTION EXPERTS

While every auction is unique, with hundreds of thousands of different types of items available, there are certain items successful sellers agree on. We talked to small business owners who do a substantial amount of their sales via eBay and other online auction services to see what they thought was important. Here's what they had to say:

Steve Weber—*http://www.webwerbooks.com*—author of *The Home Based Bookstore* recommends the following:

- *Start your auction at a penny*. People are more likely to check out listings that have a high number of bids, as they want to see what everybody else is so interested in. Starting with a low initial price will generate a lot of quick early bids.
- *Know your target audience, and list your products in appropriate categories*. Because Weber's book is of interest primarily to those who sell books, he listed it in "Wholesale Book Bulk Lots"—where book sellers go to buy books!
- *Don't worry about profit for the first six months*. You'll need that time to learn the ins and outs of the auction system.
- *Streamline operations by answering common seller questions before they're asked*. Most questions center around shipping. Address these issues in your listing.
- *Remember, it's all about taking care of the customers!* Answer their questions, and do what you have to, to make sure they're satisfied with their purchases.

Andy Schechter proprietor of a gold equipment and instrument exchange business—*http://www.golfclubexchange.com* and *http://www.instrumentexchange.com*—and expert on specialty auction sites has this advice:

- *Look for "eEnablers."* These new companies are springing up to help small businesses navigate the sometimes confusing world of online auctions. Special software packages help retailers maximize profits on specialty auction sites, by providing real-time price data and other industry specific information.

- *Work with sites that allow you to cross post.* If you list a golf club on my site, we'll help you cross post on eBay, *Overstock.com*, you name it. Similar in nature to the multiple listing format, we see in real estate, this cross posting trend will expose your products to an even wider range of customers.
- *Really do your research.* What specialty auctions are robust marketplaces? Which ones aren't so hot? You know where you'll want to be!

Lynn Dralle—*http://www.TheQueen of Acutions.com*—knows quite a bit about eBay. She's the author of *More 100 Best Things I've Sold on eBay Money Making Madness* and several other auction-focused books says:

- *Look at auctions as a way to clear out slow moving inventory.* Don't get locked into what you initially paid for the item—focus on turnover. It's better to sell six things quickly than to have dead weight sitting around your shop or home office.
- *Focus on creating a real presence on eBay.* People will get to know you, add you to their favorite seller lists. They'll visit your eBay stores and buy lots of add-on items.
- *Get the Gallery picture and avoid all the other bells and whistles.* When you list an item on eBay, why get bombarded with features. special placement? We say get the Gallery picture and avoid all the other bells and whistles.

- *Don't even attempt to sell things on eBay until you have 10 feedback points from your buyers.* Buyers tend not to buy things from a seller without feedback. Go buy 10 cheap things to create a positive rating. If someone buys from you, make sure you request their feedback. If you are a buyer yourself, your buyer's rating will enhance your reputation, too.
- *Be honest about condition.* If an item has a chip or a crack, say so. If there's a little dirt, say so. I'm hyperhonest about that type of thing, and it's never cost me a sale.
- *Ship quickly.* People get excited about finding items, and then if they have to wait and wait and wait, they get very disappointed.
- *Ship carefully.* If that means two layers of bubble wrap and tons of peanuts, do it. You don't want the item to arrive broken.

IT'S ALL WHO YOU KNOW: ONLINE COMMUNITIES

There's a great sense of community among eBay sellers. They gather in chatrooms, send each other e-mails full of friendly advice, participate in mentoring programs, even gather annually for eBay Live conventions.

This may seem counterintuitive, especially for small business owners who are accustomed to viewing other small business owners as the competition. Why in the world would you want to talk shop with sellers who are vying for the same customers you are?

It turns out that those chatrooms, e-mails, and mentoring programs actually work. Participants report markedly higher sales, better supply networks, and increased satisfaction with the auction process. It might be worth checking out, especially if you plan on making auctions an integral part of your sales structure.

Chapter 16's Essential Essentials

1. Decide what you're going to sell—existing inventory or new products.
2. Decide where you're going to sell.
3. Research your site and read the tutorial.
4. Register as a seller.
5. Write your listings.
6. List your items.
7. Make the sale.
8. Ship your items by packing and shipping carefully and quickly.
9. Provide and ask for feedback to reinforce customer relations and your reputation.

For more information on this topic, go to

www.essentialonlinesolution.com.

Chapter 17

Sell for Me

Affiliate Programs Get You on the Map

I can't stop the money from coming in even if I wanted to."

When was the last time you ever heard that statement? When you think about what that means, you start to think that it must just be an exaggeration or some off-the-cuff bragging. Then you realize there are really online businesses that actually mean it. This is the fascinating world of the affiliate program. The best part is everybody can do it.

Here is how it works. It is simply getting paid a commission for the referral or link to another site. You only get paid when that person makes a purchase; but you will continue to make a commission as long as that person buys from that supplier. Therefore you really can't stop the money from coming in.

Don't worry. You don't have to start calling all your friends to pressure them to buy from the source. You just have to place a link on your site that goes to their site. Make sure you would normally recommend the resource without a commission to the readers of your site. They will know the difference.

Associate programs are becoming so lucrative that there are now thousands of sites that have just become referral sites. These sites are just a collection of links, nothing else. Many of them are extremely profitable—after all, what are their expenses? They don't buy or sell anything; they just maintain a web site, although they must be able to attract traffic to the site. The money never stops.

Even Amazon has a referral program. Just pick the books you would recommend and Amazon helps you set up the link from your site. Anytime one of the people who come through your site buys, you get paid. (Is there a business that couldn't recommend a book to its customers? Now you can actually get paid for that recommendation. Actually, it also might motivate you to do it. The commission rate is currently at 8.5 percent. One of Rick's books gets a 5 percent royalty commission from its publisher. Amazon pays more for referring it than Rick did for writing it. Think about that.

As in many of the chapters of this book, this one could easily be a book in itself; but our purpose is to give the essentials. Let's begin with a question-and-answer format because this area of online commerce seems more of a mystery than others.

The reason it is a mystery is that this area is new and slower to develop than other areas of online commerce. Initially, the returns didn't seem significant. (Rick's favorite expression for this is: "The juice wasn't worth the squeeze.") They didn't justify the investment. The tipping point came when three elements intersected. First, more companies started to offer commissioned affiliate programs. That added two subbenefits: a blue chip company (1) endorsing and adopting this new method of marketing; and (2) more programs to select from—which meant you could tailor your program to the exact needs of your customers.

Second, commissions got bigger and longer. That means that instead of the 8.5 percent that Amazon paid, there were companies offering 50 percent or higher commissions and these commissions were paid as long as the customer bought from the resource. Some of these resources were subscription services that can go on a lifetime.

The third element is that web sites and newsletter lists became larger, which increased the possibilities of making money. When Rick's web site saw only a few hundred unique visitors a month, it didn't make sense. But when unique visitors get into the thousands, the numbers change.

Consider these numbers. If 100 people visited your site and two bought two $20 books through your link with Amazon, it means you made $1.70. Now if you had 1,000 visits and 2 percent purchased the same product, you made $11.70 from 10 visitors. Change the product to something that you would receive a $100 commission. (There are plenty of those that we will show you soon.) This means you can earn $1,000 a month. Do you see the possibilities yet? If you work hard (again, we will show the ways later in this chapter) to get just one more buyer per 100 or a 1 percent increase, you can earn an additional $500. The best part is you can have more than just one affiliate program on a site or in an e-mail.

Researching affiliates turned out to be the easiest research we did! Everyone shared their resources and methods openly. The reason? As we shared a resource, our sources also made new affiliate referrals. I know what you are thinking: "They had a vested interest, so how good could those referrals be?" Very good! Why?

Because the first rule is recommend companies that you would recommend for free. Rick loves to recommend *Elance.com*, a referral site for freelance professionals. It killed him when he found out Elance paid a $15 commission for every deal made.

Having said all of that, we make a statement that almost breaks that rule: In this book *no* affiliate programs or commissions were paid to any of the sources we recommended. No, we didn't have to do that because of Rule #1. But we never left any doubt about our motivations, recommendations, or endorsements. However, if you don't do it, you are a *liar* and a *cheat*!

Wow, what does that mean? Those are pretty strong words. Actually, they were used for shock value.

If you say your business is concerned about your clients and customers, and you don't recommend sources that can better their lives or business, then you are lying about your concern. You are also cheating them out of information that could make a difference. This isn't about just making money, it's about good business.

Let's answer some of the basic questions:

Q. Is it called an Affiliate Program or Associate Program?
A. Both. We do not see any distinction between the two names. Those terms are interchangeable.

Q. Are there any other names used for these programs?
A. Yes. Some call them by names such as Internet Affiliate Marketing, Performance Marketing, Partner Marketing, Pay-For-Performance Programs, and Referral Programs. There may be more names, but these seem to be the most popular.

Q. Are there different ways these programs work?

A. Yes, very different ways. Understand that this concept is under a big umbrella. Simply put, it is making a referral to someone who is *interested* or has a higher probability to purchase an item. The only difference is now you get paid for those referrals. We italicize "interested" because it is the difference between success and failure, which we will address after we next discuss the different types.

Q. What are the different ways?

A. • *Picture of product.* First, is the classic Amazon style, where you can have a picture of the product on your page. When someone clicks through to that product, it takes the person to the seller's site. If the prospect purchases the item, the seller pays you a commission.

• *Ad on your site.* This is a small display ad on your site and it pays as previously described.

• *Recommendation page.* This is a simple list of resources to recommend your readers. As prospects click on the resource, it takes them to the site and if they buy, you get paid.

• *In the copy.* A link is placed in web page or e-mail copy that links you to the product. This method has the advantage of an interested party who, following your line of thought, will be more apt to click on it.

• *In the copy of a third-party e-mail.* If you ask any of the savvy affiliate marketers, they agree that the best source is a referral from another business. If the business has credibility, then the recommendation goes a long way. Here another business sends an e-mail to its list recommending your product. When someone clicks through and buys, a commission is paid to the business that made the recommendation.

- *Pay per click.* This was discussed earlier as a way to draw visitors to your site. Now let's discuss it's ability to pay a commission. Instead of being paid on a transaction, pay per click pays for each visitor who clicks and accesses a site—that is, just for the click. Google, for example, gets paid when a click occurs, not when the sale occurs. The cost might only be 10 cents a click; but it adds up. It is quantity, not quality.

- *Referral pay per click.* Have you ever searched for a plumber or electrician online? The first two or three pages of results are mostly sites that are similar to the affiliate program, but with a twist. That is a referral service. This is where a site charges a fee to be part of the service. If you do a search for just about any profession today, you generally go through page after page of referral sites. Every industry has them—plumbers, electricians, contractors, builders, as well as graphic designers, consultants, dentists, lawyers, and speakers. These sites promise their member businesses work in return for a fee. (Some sites will also want to be paid for any work that is contracted.) We have these services both as buyer and seller. Rick used *Elance.com* for freelance graphics people and researchers. He was thrilled with their service. Great people and a job done right at an affordable price.

Rick has not been as successful with the referral services for which he paid because they were new services that had no track record. Here is the message to be learned about these referral services. First, understand that they are only selling a listing on a web site and a promise of business because of their search engines positioning. They generally pay their salespeople very lucrative first-time commissions. Therefore, you can get pressure from some real sharpies. Find out how long they have been in business, interview users of the service, and find out how long they have stayed with the service. If it's new, it generally won't work for awhile. Don't be the pioneer—it rarely pays. Wait a little bit until the service gets established, which might even be a few years. That is a word of caution: Be careful and look for guarantees. Check out its Google rank. If the service isn't in the top 20, *run*. Sure there are exceptions, but why bother?

The bottom line is lots of buyers and sellers are paying lots of money to create this new industry. Make sure they are not just successful because they sold a lot of unhappy customers. Let the buyer beware (and be warned).

Q. What do you mean by "interested people?"

A. Interested people are at the heart of any successful affiliate program. Getting them that way is what Ken Evoy, the author of the *Affiliate Masters Course* and the founder of *www.SiteSell.com*, would call a presell. He is one of the most successful site developers on the planet today and is a very shrewd marketer. If you are serious about this business, you will automatically check out his site and learn about his *free* course. It will presell you.

Putting up links to unrelated products only hurts your credibility. When visitors click to the desired site, they have their guard up. Ken refers to "tightly niched theme-based content." For example, Rick is a retail specialist, so links to anything that relate to retailing make sense. Rick loses some of his credibility when nonretail people visit his site. This book, *Online Solutions*, is a more universal topic than just retailing and it is just as important to the general contractor as to the retailer. However, if a contractor ever went to Rick's retail site after reading *Online Solutions*, he or she would be turned off because the tight niche doesn't apply to that type of business.

Is that right? *No*. Rick wrote the *Retail Business Kit for Dummies* that sold almost 50,000 copies worldwide. He is the King in The

World of retailing—but over 80 percent of that book could easily be perceived as a general small business book. Is it right that Rick is sometimes seen as an expert in one field and not in another? Yes it is right because it is about the way the customer perceives us.

Q. You mentioned SiteSell and Ken Evoy. Who else is an Essential?
A. *Allan Gardyne—http://www.Associateprograms.com*—is a great source with listings of possible affiliate programs that you can get involved in. Make sure you read his "18-Step Approach to Affiliate" success. *Refer-it.com* is a classic to use but the big Kahuna, the biggest of them all is AdSense from Google. There are different ways to make money with AdSense from searches to having AdSense advertise other business on your site and get paid for the advertising. AdSense has wonderful tutorials and will become a major part of your affiliate business.

LifetimeCommissions.com is an interesting site to check out because we get a feel for the different types of products that have enormous potential. Also *RealQuest.com* and *AffiliatesAlert.com* are interesting sites to review. *http://www.partnercentric.com* is another good site to review.

Q. What are directories and how do they work?
A. A directory page is just a list of links. *Business.com* is a good example but others are *botw.com, WowDirectory.com, Yahoo!, DMOZ.com, Gimpsy.com, Geniusfind.com,* and *LookSmart. com*. These are all places you can advertise your site.

Q. My site doesn't get that much traffic. Should I even bother?
A. Yes, because you don't just do it for the money. You are doing it to better serve your customer. You are providing a service to

them plus you will be perceived as the expert or the resource. That is a good thing.

Q. What are the best programs to get involved in?
A. Associate with the types of business that will add credibility and support to your brand. If you are known for the different and unusual, then you should seek out different and unusual links. The constant theme is: How can it help your reader? Look for the win, win, wins.

Q. Where else can you go to find programs?
A. Just go to any site you are interested in and look for its affiliate program. You will be shocked when you realize how many have them. (Do you have one?)

Q. How does it work?
A. Each affiliate will work a little differently but the concept is pretty basic and they will all have a tutorial or set of instructions to follow. After the first couple you will get the hang of it or just have your webmaster tackle it for you.

Q. What do misspellings have to do with anything?
A. We have discussed the power of misspelled words and how we can end up in places we never expected. It is even more powerful here. Remember the old expression "garbage in, garbage out"? Change it to "garbage in, gold out." If someone—searching for dance supplies for his or her daughter—types too fast and searches for "ance supplies," and you have created a simple site with "*ance-supplies.com*," he or she might end up on your page. If you create a site of referrals for dance supplies, you can make money while you are sleeping. Just don't tell your seventh grade English teacher how you are making money from spelling things wrong.

Q. What does it all mean?

A. It means that there is a new world that is less than seven years old where the streets are *paved with gold*. There were many settlers who sailed across the Atlantic to find those streets. Some were disappointed because they found no gold on the streets; but others saw opportunities worth more than a solid gold street. Some saw limitless opportunities, while others complained that they had to work for their gold. Others tried to cut corners, even lie or exaggerate, to find their gold.

Who worked hard and built solid businesses succeeded.

Don't look for the worthless, get rich quick, "fooled ya" way of doing business. Do it the right way. Create worthwhile valuable content that people want to read and then service them with the best referrals you can make to make their lives better and their businesses grow. They will be more than happy to click on the sites you recommend and thank you for doing it. Then the money will follow in quantities you can't even imagine.

Then do it again, and again, and again.

Welcome to the Gold Rush.

Chapter 17's Essential Essentials

1. Never recommend something you don't believe in. It only hurts you later.
2. First have a site with content so that your recommendation means something.
3. Be careful in choosing directories and services. Only a few really work.

Chapter 17's Essential Essentials, *continued*

4. Misspellings are more powerful than you realize.
5. Not all affiliate programs are structured the same way.
6. Yes, there really is a place you can make money forever!

For more information on this topic, go to

www.essentialonlinesolution.com.

Chapter 18

Bringing It All Together

After all of the planning, writing, rejecting, modifying, editing, interviewing, verifying, discussing and even arguing, we have reached the wrapup, the last chapter. But is it really?

No!

It might be the end of this book, but it's the start of a new world. At this writing, the World Wide Web is approaching its 11th birthday. In that time, millionaires have been made, fortunes have been lost, and the dot-com bust was a necessary adjustment toward reality. What is more important is that thousands of unknown faces have been making a living with a form of commerce that didn't exist when they were born.

We hope we have helped to launch new businesses, helped people to build existing business, or uncover potential no one realized they had. We wanted to show you a way to succeed, the essential things you need to succeed. We have simplified the process as much as we could, and we believe we have delivered the true *essentials* of doing business online. Some may challenge our positions and preferences and our interpretation of what is and is not essential. We can assure you of only one thing: No one could have challenged those beliefs more than we did. We researched, tested, tried, asked opinions, wrote about it, and then reviewed it later. That is the beauty of the online world. It keeps on challenging us and keeps us up to date and in a constant learning mode—and that's *good*!

We had nearly completed a chapter when we discovered new research that set us off in another direction only to come full circle after more crucial testing and evaluating. That phenomenon seemed to repeat itself over and over and is a lesson to be learned. The latest and greatest must always be reviewed, tested, tried, but change for the sake of new is not productive. New is important—but is the benefit worth the learning *curve* and implementation period? As Rick likes to say, "Is the juice worth the squeeze?"

The online world is truly a phenomenon that takes us places we never thought we could go. It's a world of *wows*. Yet the web site has become the anti-*wow*. The online world is a world where convenience rules and time and understandability become the currency of the medium. For this reason, we wrote the book constantly asking: "Is that the easiest way to understand? Can we make it simpler?" But the question we asked 50 times a day was, "Is that an essential? If so, WHY?"

So let's review our five steps, remind you of the essentials, and reinforce the ideas you have adopted. The one thing you should have observed by now is that the *essential solution* is constantly evolving and changing. Yet it fits into a structure that can accommodate hypergrowth and change. Our essential solution is supported by five steps outlined in the following sections.

STEP ONE: UNCOVER THE POSSIBILITIES

The first step in uncovering possibilities is knowing where we are at and trying to grasp the almost limitless possibilities.

Look at the history of e-commerce, the good, the bad and the ugly and relate it to the present day. What are the possibilities of online commerce for you? What have others achieved, what can you achieve, and what is yet to be achieved from your perspective on the world? With all the money, power, brains, and experience of the software giants, how could two young kids create a company like Google right under the giants' collective noses? They saw the possibilities from their perspective, from their experience and view of the world.

What Google did and what we must do is to look at where you have been and where you can go to uncover the newest, latest, and greatest. Google created the tool for the rest of us to use. The more we learn, the more we want, and the more we need to evaluate what is right for us. We need to understand our *desired results* and be willing to adjust and be flexible to the changes in technology.

It is important to understand why people buy online before you try to sell to them. If the buyer is only concerned about convenience and speed, then why are we constantly offering price incentives? Part of uncovering the possibilities is understanding the online motivations for buying that differ from other buying motivations.

The last part of this step is to realize the five levels of online commerce and commitment. Two of these levels are usually transitional levels for businesses that are growing and expanding. Two levels are places we may want to stay and live at for years. We can be very successful there. But the top level is not the top of the mountain. It is the climber trying to reach the top that is always 100 yards away. It is the endless quest for the latest and the best that *works* and works for the business.

Part of understanding the possibilities is knowing what will make us happy when we get there. Some people are happy with a new Chevy while others need the BMW. Both will get you where you want to go. Actually there are many businesses happy with the Chevy level of e-commerce and drive BMWs with their success. You might not need another level for your business.

Uncovering the possibilities is about uncovering what is right for you, what can be done, what has been done, what should be avoided, and where can you go to be on the cutting edge of technology. It is about the level of commitment needed for you to achieve your desired results.

STEP TWO: BUILDING PRACTICAL, POWERFUL, PROFESSIONAL WEB SITES THAT WORK

This is command central, the home office, mission control, the heart of online commerce, the front door to your business. We know online commerce is more than that—but the web site is the big cog wheel.

This step goes through four stages of better understanding your web site.

The first stage is better understanding the front door of your online business, uncovering the myths of the e-commerce, and learning new key expressions to online success:

- Know your *desired result*.
- Make sure you are in alignment with your business.
- Identify what *desired actions* you want your reader to take.
- The power of the misspelled word.
- The power of the name.
- The stage of knowing what the winning sites have.
- The Ps to Profit—Pull them in. Prove the point. Purchase.
- Convenience—it's the tipping point of the web. Make it easy to use.

- The 8-Second Rule—visitors to your site must discover a match within the first eight seconds of viewing your page or they are gone.
- The First Page Rule—because of the 8-Second Rule, the first page that the visitor views had better be all about that prospective customer and the benefit to them.
- Minimum level of professionalism—it's the contra *wow*. Flash introduction pages and the like don't work. Most people will hit the *Skip Intro* button. The more you spend does not equate to more online success.
- Specialize—have multiple sites where each one specializes in different products of your business. People search for specialists. Treat yourself as one.
- Sticky—make your site sticky. Copy, headlines, pictures, and free stuff are the leading sticky vehicles.
- Read your statistics and know who visits your site, how long they stay, and why they leave.

We then move to the structure of the site, learning the following essentials:

- Eliminate clutter from your site. Eliminate choices.
- Learn the killer designs you can use in your web site.
- Creating simple layouts.
- Web designers and webmasters—what roles do they play and who do you need?
- Templates and styles—what's the difference?
- What choices of category navigation buttons are there?
- What seven categories are you selecting and why?
- The Saab effect affects us all. How does it affect you?
- Map and plan your steps to web site creation.

The last stage in this step is actually reviewing various sites, seeking the best and the not so good, and how we need to duplicate what we did in the book. These are just some of the findings:

- Break your offering down into logical chunks of information.
- Take your customer age into account when planning the readability of your site.
- Don't focus on the price as the first thing.
- Personalize your site in every way you can.
- An unprofessional web site hurts you rather than helps you even if you have a high Google ranking.
- If you received an award, place a picture of it on your home page.
- Make technology work for your customers to ease buying online.
- Have an easy-to-find and use navigation bar.
- Offer a contest that links your business with a nationally celebrated specialty holiday or week.

STEP THREE: CREATING EXPERT STATUS

This book is geared for small business, and one of the most powerful tools that the small business person has is an expertise or specialty. Even if you are a business that is focused on price, you must justify your lower price and that is done with expertise. This might seem like an unusual step; but we want to do business with people who are the specialists and experts. That's why this step is all about ways to achieve expert status in the mind of our customer. We believe there are three key elements of this step:

1. E-mail marketing
2. The blog
3. Podcasting

E-Mail Marketing

E-mail marketing is powerful because it allows us to get closer to our customers and gives us an opportunity to position ourselves as experts. This medium is an essential of online commerce because it combines image building, brand building, and promotional opportunities all rolled up into one medium. The goal is to share knowledge and create a benefit to the reader in every e-mail marketing campaign you do. The lessons to learn and use are:

- Use the same standard format every time.
- Designate a consistent day of the week or month that you send out your e-mail campaign.
- Implement a name collection strategy.
- Align your e-mail marketing with your company look and feel.
- Be current with all laws concerning opt-in and -out procedures.
- Copy is king.
- Use modified long copy when writing your e-mail marketing message.
- Learn and use the data from your conversion rate to build sales.
- Link to the page on your site where you want action taken.

The Blog

The blog is becoming an extension of e-mail marketing. It is a place where you can interact with your customers, serve to reiterate information in your newsletter, or just a place to voice your opinion to the world. We treat this as one of the most essential essentials.

It is important to remember that the blog is a web site and is not limited to what you can do with it. The articles can be short or long. They can be daily, weekly, or monthly. The reasons every business must have a blog are:

- It costs nothing but time.
- It positions you as an expert.
- It brings you closer to your customers.
- It is a great place to store newsletters.
- It becomes a powerful traffic builder to your web site.

Podcasting

"Beam me up, Scottie" was once sci-fi jargon. Cell phones have become a major player in personal communication. However, we have taken mobile personalization into the world of entertainment and education. Newsletters are now being downloaded onto small MP3 players and listened to or watched during exercise, on the train, or wherever you choose. When you hear the words *entertainment* and *education*, red flags should signal business opportunity. These are the lessons to be learned:

- Send your messages in story form.
- Link stories with great content about your service or product.
- Choose two or three podcast sites to list your podcast.
- Review the Seven Scary Podcasting No-Nos.
- Place your podcast on your web site or link to the podcast from your web site.
- Connect your podcast to at least two RSS feeds.

Step Three was about creating expert status. We believe that it is an essential because it is the fertile ground for differentiation. It is the place where we can compete effectively and a place where big business rarely succeeds.

STEP FOUR: CREATING THE BUZZ
WITH CLICKS AND CLENDS

We know where we want to go, we have built a powerful web site, our e-mails, newsletters, blogs, and podcasts are working fine—but they work very slowly. You want to make things happen *now*! That's why this step is so important. It has four components:

1. Web positioning or search engine optimization
2. Pay per click advertising
3. Traditional and new uses of technology to advertise
4. Creating word-of-mouth (viral marketing) and advertising the *clend*—click and send

Web Positioning or Search Engine Optimization

Not to make web positioning an essential is like having a party and not telling everyone where the party is going to be. The art and science of getting a web site positioned so that it comes up high in the search engines is essential for any successful campaign.

- Choose your keyword phrases.
- Make sure your web site content is rich with your keywords.
- Load your title, header, and subheader tags with your keyword phrase.
- Write and submit articles to gain organically grown links.
- Submit to the key search engines and directories we recommended.
- Remember it will take three to four months to see a difference.
- Be sure to track to make sure your web positioning has made a difference in your hits and conversions to sales.

We believe in web positioning but it is quickly becoming replaced with strong pay per click campaigns that can ensure being seen—but there is a fee involved.

Pay Per Click Advertising

This is what made Google's founders and investors very rich. It is just a simple tool to advertise to the people who are searching for specific words. So the steps within this step are:

- What words do people use to search for what you sell?
- Define how much you are willing to spend per month.
- Decide what search engines you want to use—Google is the biggest and best.
- Write your ad copy using four to six killer words.
- Test two or three ads at the same time to know which ad is best.
- Track the ad statistics to know the impact of your ad on your business.
- Tweak, tweak, tweak your ad words, your search engines, and your copy for the best results.

Traditional and New Uses of Technology to Advertise

The next step in this step is not ignoring traditional forms of advertising and embracing the new age forms such as AdSense. We can't disregard successful advertising methods and we must remember that Amazon, Monster, and eBay still use nontraditional methods.

- Make sure your web address appears in all of your advertising, signage, and e-mails.
- Consider banner ads as part of your marketing strategy.
- Explore banner ad exchange programs.

- Popup ads might work but be prepared for backlash—not everyone likes them!
- Investigate the use of AdSense as buyer and seller and see if it makes sense for your business.
- Service businesses and any business that do well with traditional yellow pages should consider listing with Super Pages.
- Consider using DoubleClick when you become serious about online advertising. It's the difference between knowing and not knowing what works. It takes the guesswork out of addressing.

Creating Word-of-Mouth (Viral Marketing) and Advertising the Clend (Click and Send)

This is where we get very opinionated about the concept of viral marketing. It's word-of-mouth; it's WOMA. But if we want WOMA, we have to give people something to talk about. This step explores what people talk about and how you start the buzz.

- Understand your pass-along rate.
- Understand the power of FREE.
- Touch the emotions of your audience.
- If you want WOMA, then give people something to talk about.

STEP FIVE—SELL, SELL, SELL

This last step is the optional essential. You can live happily ever after without this step; but there are more people who live happily ever after who use this step. It has just two elements. But those elements are so powerful that books have been written about them. It is the World of eBay and Rick's favorite, the Affiliate World. eBay is for everyone today, from collectors to off-price merchants, from tire distributors to used tires that the neighbor is trying to sell. These are the key elements of eBay.

- Auctions are more than just eBay; there are other auction sites.
- Explore specialty auction sites.
- Read the tutorials. They generally contain most of the information you need to get started.
- Register as a seller.
- It's all in the copy of the description.
- Make good use of keywords and photographs.
- eBay Stores—explore the possibilities.
- Don't lose prospects over the basics. Accept charge cards and offer user-friendly shipping.
- Positive feedback does count here.

The Affiliate Program

This means getting paid for referrals—but it opens the door for so many possibilities. Recommending affiliates—or associates—can lead to a separate stream of income, and it can become a subscription service as well. Look at how you can select a plumber or electrician online. You will find that they often belong to a referral services. Dentists, lawyers, and freelance artists and writers also take advantage of this type of service.

Referral services go by the same principle as the affiliate program. The only difference is in the way people get paid. The affiliate program pays a commission for people who are referred and purchase something. It is an essential because, when done right, your customers and clients perceive it as great customer service. The keepers are:

- This system allows you to make money forever. You can't stop it even if you wanted.
- Never recommend for money something you wouldn't recommend for free.
- The program is as good as the company you are doing business with.
- Small commissions might not be worth the recommendation.
- Look for programs that pay lifetime commissions.
- The best referral programs are comprised of items that are purchased regularly.

As we wrote this recap, it triggered interviews, articles, and discussions. But what it did the most was reinforce what we did and the steps we selected to make the *Essential Online Solution*. These five steps cover multiple ways of creating and building an online business. The concepts we talked about are tested and proven; but they not old fashioned. The concepts may vary with the advent of new technology. These essential steps, nevertheless, will always remain the essentials.

Enjoy the ride. Visit us online at *essentialonlinesolutions.com* for even more information. There will be people just like yourself who will turn our words into action and action into more money than you ever could have imagined. So write to us and let us know if you are one of the many who have already made your stake in the gold rush online. The time is now!

INDEX